D1452640

The Resurrection of Man

BY THE SAME AUTHOR

The Easter Enigma

The Pattern of Matins and Evensong

Meet the Prayer Book

The Miracles and the Resurrection (with I. T. Ramsey, G. H. Boobyer, F. N. Davey and Henry J. Cadbury)

Experiment in Worship

The Churchman's Companion (with D. W. Cleverley Ford, D. N. Sargent and Reginald Cant)

Declaring the Faith: The Printed Word (with Dewi Morgan)

Crisis for Confirmation (editor)

Sharing in One Bread

MOWBRAYS LIBRARY OF THEOLOGY

The Resurrection of Man

Christian teaching on life after death

Michael Perry

Archdeacon of Durham

MOWBRAYS LONDON & OXFORD

© *Michael Charles Perry 1975*

First Published 1975
by A. R. Mowbray & Co. Ltd
The Alden Press, Osney Mead
Oxford OX2 0EG

ISBN 0 264 66254 7

Printed in Great Britain
at the Alden Press, Oxford

237
P429

203567

Introduction to Mowbrays Library of Theology

The last quarter of the twentieth century is a good time for the Christian Church to take stock of its beliefs. In the course of the century, Christian theology has had many challenges to meet—and has itself not remained unchanged by the encounter. Society has become more pluralist and less committed; dogmatism is at a discount. Christianity has had to survive in a climate which regards its beliefs as matters of opinion rather than of fact, and in a world not readily convinced of their relevance either to public politics or private morals. Within the faith (and particularly in the sixties of the century) there have been radical questionings of almost every aspect of doctrine.

Despite all this, there are signs that people are more willing now than they were a decade or so ago to listen to more constructive voices. Christians need to state how they can—as men of their own age and culture, and as heirs to the radical ferment of ideas which characterised the mid-century—articulate a faith in God, Father, Son and Holy Spirit, hold convictions about the nature of man and his destiny, and show the relevance of belief to conduct. The contributors to this series think it their duty to give as plain and straightforward a statement as is compatible with their intellectual integrity of what the Christian faith is, and how it can be honestly and meaningfully expressed today.

Christian faith has always been the faith of a community. It is therefore necessary to 'earth' such an articulation in terms of a particular community of Christians. So the contributors to this series are all Anglicans, confident that theirs is a particular expression of the universal faith which still merits serious consideration. The series therefore aims to reflect, not only themes of interest to all Christians at all times, but also particular aspects of Christian theology which are currently exercising the Church of England in congregations and Synods. And, since there will always be rival religions and ideologies competing for men's allegiance, we need to explore their claims and ask what the attitude of Anglicans is towards them. But that the Church has a faith which is worth stating and that it is a faith to live by, is a conviction shared by every contributor.

Contents

In memory of
CHARLIE PERRY
my father in Adam

and

IAN RAMSEY
a father in Christ

who passed from life into life
30 November and 6 October 1972

Preface

TEN years ago, I thought this book would be quickly finished. I had preached a course of Lent sermons on the subjects with which it deals (at All Saints' Margaret Street and St Mary's Primrose Hill) and had revised and polished them for a similar course the following year at St Mary's Hitchin. Then my work on the publishing side of the SPCK showed me why it was that midwives so seldom had children of their own, and a move to Durham gave me an insight into how all-absorbing could be what St Paul referred to as 'the care of all the churches'. It was only an invitation from Richard Mulkern to edit the series of which this volume is one which gave sufficient urgency to the task and enabled me to be firm with myself and set aside time enough to complete it. I am convinced, however, that the time taken in bringing the book to birth has helped it to be a better one than a more youthful essay would have been; but I am even more convinced that another ten years' reflection would have improved it even more. I would (for instance) have wanted to write much more fully about many aspects of the subject. Whole books have been written around the themes of each of the chapters, and there is a great danger of superficiality when so rigorously compressing *multum in parvo*. Nevertheless, I believe there is room for a treatment within the covers of a single short book of a matter which concerns every one of us who is going to die.

Despite the exigencies of space, I have deliberately made room for illustrative material and discussion of the data of psychical research on a scale which is greater than that which might be expected of a book of this length. There are several reasons for this. I believe that this material is not well enough known amongst Christians and its significance is often misjudged even by theologians, probably through lack of familiarity with the field. I also believe the material is important in itself, and have so maintained during the quarter of a century in which I have kept up an interest in the subject. The right balance between credulity and scepticism is hard to achieve; the reader must judge for himself whether I have been successful.

There have been several occasions on which I have previously written on kindred topics, and I am grateful to various editors and publishers for allowing me to use and adapt material originally written for a different readership. The editor of the *Expository Times* has given his permission for the adaptation of material from issues dated November 1963, February 1974 and March 1974; the editor of the *Franciscan* has been likewise generous over permission to make use of part of an article I wrote for his number of March 1968; and Messrs Faber & Faber Ltd have allowed me to re-work material which originally appeared as part of chapter 8 of *The Easter Enigma* (1959). I have also quoted from other writers, sometimes quite extensively, and would like to thank the following for allowing me to do so:

Abingdon Press (J. Knox, *Christ and the Hope of Glory*);

W. H. Allen & Co. Ltd (J. A. Pike, *The Other Side*);

James Clarke and William Collins Sons & Co. Ltd (J. A. T. Robinson, *In the End, God*);

William Collins Sons & Co. Ltd (C. S. Lewis, *The Weight of Glory*);

Darton, Longman & Todd Ltd (G. O'Collins, *The Easter Jesus*);

J. M. Dent & Sons Ltd (Everyman edition of Plato's *Timaeus*);

Hodder & Stoughton Ltd (Arnold Toynbee *et al.*, *Man's Concern with Death*);

Hutchinson Publishing Group Ltd (J. D. Pearce-Higgins and G. S. Whitby, eds., *Life, Death and Psychical Research*);

Lutterworth Press Ltd (W. Schneemelcher, ed., *New Testament Apocrypha*);

Macmillan, London and Basingstoke (J. Hick, *Evil and the God of Love*);

New Christian Publications Ltd (*Christian*, vol. 1, no. 1);
Oxford University Press (J. Baillie, *And the Life Everlasting*);
Penguin Books Ltd (*Penguin Classics* editions of Bede, *A History of the English Church and People* and Augustine, *Confessions*);
SCM Press Ltd (C. F. Evans, *Resurrection and the New Testament*; W. Marxsen, *The Resurrection of Jesus of Nazareth*; J. A. T. Robinson, *Honest to God*; J. V. Taylor, *The Primal Vision*; M. F. Wiles, *The Remaking of Christian Doctrine*);
Sidgwick & Jackson (W. H. Salter, *Zoar*);
SPCK (*Prayer and the Departed*).

My thanks are also due to the Council of the Society for Psychical Research for permission to quote extensively from material published in the *Journal* and *Proceedings* of the Society and from the Myers Memorial Lectures by Chancellor Garth Moore and Sir Cyril Burt.

Unless otherwise stated, biblical quotations have been taken from the *New English Bible*, second edition, ©1970, by permission of Oxford and Cambridge University Presses.

MICHAEL PERRY

Durham, January 1975

1 Facing death

A FEW years ago, I was taking part in a Brains Trust, and one of the questions was about heart transplants and 'spare-parts surgery'. I mentioned a friend of mine who had willed his body to a teaching hospital to be used in anatomical studies, and the very idea so revolted a woman journalist on the panel that she felt she had to protest. 'I could never do a thing like that', she said. 'I cannot imagine myself dead and I don't want to try.'

Even in our emancipated century, there are subjects which are too embarrassing to be raised in company, and death is one of them. It is simply not good taste to talk about it, and even our jokes are nervous and ill-at-ease. 'Die, my dear Doctor,' said Viscount Palmerston with his final breath, 'that's the last thing I shall do!'; and we feel that the levity is just too near the bone to be comfortable. We are very unlike the Victorians, who were open, enlightened and emancipated. They may have been prudes about birth, but we are worse prudes about death, the great unmentionable.

Why? After all, every one of us has to die. If we have done away with our embarrassment about birth, surely we can be clinical and unemotional about the other end of our life on earth? No; and the reason may be that though the *fact* of death is known, its *mystery* is not. Here we must distinguish between two fears: the fear of the act of dying and the fear of being dead.

Perhaps we fear the act of dying because we are cowards about pain. If so, it may help us to know that—as far as we can tell—the act of dying is (in normal circumstances) remarkably painless.[1] There may be pain to be borne beforehand, in the unwillingness of the body to submit to the indignities of disease or injury; but when that struggle is over and the link between consciousness and the physical body can no longer be maintained, all the evidence is that the slipping away is no more of a terror than the drift into oblivion that we painlessly accomplish every night when we fall asleep. More often, the fear of the act of dying is a psychological rather than a physical one. To die is to lose control of one's self, to surrender, to hand over to a process over which one has no control. It is the involuntariness of death which can terrify the person who finds it hard to 'let himself go'.

The fear of being dead, however, is of another order than the fear of dying. It is the fear of the unknown. In the words of Hamlet,

> the dread of something after death,
> The undiscover'd country from whose bourn
> No traveller returns, puzzles the will,
> And makes us rather bear those ills we have,
> Than fly to others that we know not of.[2]

What makes death so dreadful, and makes us live our lives in a great conspiracy of silence, trying to forget that they must one day end, is not that we *know* that we are going to be snuffed out like a candle, or that we *know* that there is something on the other side of the experience. We are, rather, terrified because we do *not* know.[3] If we could be certain—even if we could be sure that what lay beyond would be unpleasant—we would not be worried. We can face up to anything once we are certain what it is. What J. B. Priestley has called the 'consensus opinion' of our contemporaries is that 'we know the processes of birth and death, the *how* of them, but not the why of them; we have entrances and exits without meaning, as if compelled to take part in a bad play.'[4] And this is an uncomfortable situation to be in. We demand scientific knowledge and a guaranteed certainty, and we expect any religion worth the name to give it us in relation to the prospects of mankind after death.

That is, perhaps, why—although people are embarrassed to *talk* about the matter—they are ready to read books on death and dying and on whether anything lies beyond them. There has certainly been a spate of such books in recent years. It is not only the already convinced who read them. It is quite possible to be a regular churchgoer and yet be uncertain about whether there is a life beyond death. This should not surprise us, nor should we think it reprehensible. Many people go to church (or read religious books), not because they have answered all the problems of life but because they have *not*. They may have lived for years with an unresolved uncertainty at the centre of their lives and have never had the courage either to admit it or to bring it out into the open for rational examination or discussion.

There must be many people like this. According to a survey carried out in 1974 by the Opinion Research Centre for BBC 1's 'Anno Domini' programme, one person in four is uncertain whether or not to believe in life after death. Yet almost everyone has some kind of a religious service at his funeral and would be shocked at the thought of being 'put away' without ceremony.[5] People may not be convinced, but they like to play safe. They are rather like the devout old lady who used to bow her head in church every time the devil was mentioned, 'because', as she said, 'civility costs you nothing, and you never know . . .'.

The demand for certainty is not all that modern. Thirteen hundred years ago some of our Northumbrian ancestors were gathered in the court of King Edwin to debate whether they should accept the new teaching which the Christian missionaries under Paulinus had brought over. In the course of the debate, one of the king's chief men had this to say:

Your Majesty, when we compare the present life of man on earth with that time of which we have no knowledge, it seems to me like the swift flight of a single sparrow through the banqueting-hall where you are sitting at dinner on a winter's day with your thanes and counsellors. In the midst there is a comforting fire to warm the hall; outside, the storms of winter rain or snow are raging. This sparrow flies swiftly in through one door of the hall, and out through another. While he is inside, he is safe from the winter storms; but after a few moments of comfort, he vanishes from sight into the wintry world from which he came. Even so, man appears on earth for a little while; but of what went before this life or of what follows, we know nothing. Therefore, if this new teaching has brought any more certain knowledge, it seems only right that we should follow it.[5]

Is there a faith which can tell us anything about the mystery of the unseen, about what went before and what follows this earthly life of ours? That is a universal question, as real now as then. The answer we give to it will affect not only our attitude to death, but also our attitude to life.

It makes a difference to our attitude to life because, if we are sure of our destination, we can get the perspective of our lives right. The purpose of knowledge about what may happen after death is, in the words of a book which had a tremendous vogue in the early years of this century,[7] 'to help us to live rightly in this world, not to satisfy our curiosity about the other'. An interest in the next world does not dull our appreciation of the things of this present life, nor does it minimise its importance to us; rather the reverse. During an illness, John Donne, Dean of St Paul's in the seventeenth century, wrote these words:

> Since I am coming to that Holy roome,
>   Where, with thy Quire of Saints for evermore,
> I shall be made thy Musique; As I come
>   I tune the instrument here at the dore,
>   And what I must doe then, thinke here before.

Of course, the instrument which is to be made God's music would be better tuned earlier than on one's death-bed, but the principle may be granted. Our eternal destiny affects our whole life. It is the perspective within which each earthly action is seen in all its seriousness and importance. If we expect to spend eternity in God's presence, we shall want to cultivate his company here and now as well. And, since God's care is universal, Christian action is properly concerned with our present human bodily conditions, with politics and humanitarianism and love for people. Furthermore, the man who is certain of his eternal direction will be capable of rejoicing in God now and of leading a joyful and relaxed Christian life.

The eternal perspective also affects the way in which we face death. There are many possible attitudes. We can be (though I think very few of us actually are) hard-headed materialists who take death for granted and say there is no need to make any fuss about it. Or we can be like the journalist we mentioned at the beginning of this chapter, who found it unthinkable. That is the attitude of the ostrich; the attitude of a song popularised by Eartha Kitt in the 1950s which proclaimed that

> If I can't take it with me when I go,
> I just ain't gonna go.

Or we may rail against the inevitability of death, though this is not very realistic. After all, the gates of death are not likely to close as a result of our complaints.

Some people, of course, actively welcome it; either in the dreadful way in which a suicide sees death as the lesser of two evils, or in the somewhat romanticised way in which, when life gets so much on top of us, we think a cessation of its never-ending activity would be a blessing. Keats was at times 'half in love with easeful death' and so probably—though expressing himself more robustly and with a great deal more theological sophistication—was St Paul when, writing to his friends at Philippi, he expressed his preference for departing to be with Christ, but realised that he still had a job to do on earth which, though often wearying, was his inescapable duty (Phil. 1.23 ff.). In most cases, the real cure for feeling this way is a good long holiday, after which the inclination is likely to be taken much less seriously.

Another attitude towards death is to trivialise it, like those American undertakers satirised in Evelyn Waugh's *The Loved One* or pilloried in Jessica Mitford's *The American Way of Death*, who try to glamourise corpses and aim to make death appear something less serious than it really is. I am not so sure that the popular version of St Francis of Assisi's *Canticle of the Sun* does not do that:

> And thou, most kind and gentle death,
> Waiting to hush our latest breath,
>   O praise him, alleluia![8]

St Francis himself, singing on his death-bed where he lay in agony with his blind and cauterised eyes, was Christian realist enough not to be so sentimental. A sterner translation of his words is that made by Crawford Burkitt:[9]

> Be praised, my Lord, for our Sister Bodily Death,
> From whom none can escape that has drawn breath.
> 'Woe to those dying in mortal sin!' He saith.
> Blest those who find that in Thy Holy Will
> The second Death to them will bring no ill.

Yes, death is not to be defied, or ignored, or trivialised, or sentimentalised; it is to be faced. Death is serious, but it is the contention of the Christian faith that we should be able to face it with confidence. Not without fear, for we are men. John Bunyan tells us that there was a wide and deep and cold river between the pilgrims' way and the celestial city; and Christian and Hopeful waded it together. Christian had a rough time of it, and began to sink.

> And with that a great darkness and horror fell upon Christian, so that he could not see before him. . . . Hopeful, therefore, here had much ado to keep his brother's head above water; yea, sometimes he would be quite gone down, and then, ere a while, he would rise up again half dead.

But he won through, and found his way to the celestial city.

The Christian claim is that what is required is not the bravado which makes light of death, but the confidence that all its terrors (genuine though they may be) are of no *real* account to one who knows who will be his companion. That is why the Christian ought not to thank anyone who tries to keep from him the knowledge that this journey must shortly be his lot; and this is the Christian's answer to those terrors we mentioned earlier, the terrors of 'letting go' and submitting to the inevitable. Falling in love (and notice the very metaphor we use to describe the experience), from the first stirrings of the emotion to its consummation in the marital act, requires a similar willingness to lose control and relax in giving one's self wholly to the trusted partner. Christian dying is a consummation of the act of falling in love with him whom we have learnt to trust during a lifetime's courting. Just as the act of love may be terrifying, so may the act of dying—in its very loss of control. But remember of whom we are disciples. We follow not Socrates, but Christ. Socrates might go to his death, calmly discoursing of immortality over a cup of hemlock; but Jesus in Gethsemane, pouring out strong tears and crying, with sweat standing out on his forehead like great drops of blood, is the one who has gone before, and there is no doubt who will be the more appropriate companion for us timorous mortals who start and shrink to cross the narrow sea. We may be frightened of the unknown, but like children in the dark, reaching out a hand to clasp our reassuring father, we can face anything in the company of someone we trust.

I said to the man who stood at the Gate of the Year, 'Give me a light that I may tread safely into the unknown.' And he replied, 'Go out into the darkness, and put your hand into the Hand of God. That shall be to you better than light, and safer than a known way.'⁹

Fine words; but are they true? The rest of this book will be an attempt to look at the evidence, to state the Christian case (for it is often misunderstood, or rejected through being presented in caricature) and to see whether reasonable men today ought to be prepared to accept it.

2 How can we know?

WHAT kind of evidence might enable us to settle the question of whether death is the end? In this chapter, we will see how far a reasonable case may be made for human survival after death without bringing either religious presuppositions or empirical facts into play.

We must first ask what it is we are talking about when we refer to 'survival after death'. There is a minor difficulty right at the start. On the one hand, most people who believe in any kind of survival believe that we are in for some surprises when we actually begin to experience it, so we must be careful not to lay down exactly what it is we are thinking to demonstrate before we begin trying to demonstrate it. On the other hand, unless we have *some* idea of what it is that our arguments are tending towards, we shall probably have rather an unprofitable time. The best way out of this dilemma seems to be for the moment to define 'survival' in minimal terms—that is, to say 'whatever else survival might involve, this at least would seem to be part of it'—so that what we have in mind can be modified and bodied out as our investigation begins to give flesh to the skeleton.

The minimal definition of survival with which we can begin is 'a continuity of self-awareness despite the fact of death'. This definition has already put out of court two ways in which 'survival' is commonly believed in. The first, which will not long detain us, is the way in which people claim that men survive through the influence they have had on the world. A man survives in his children; Shakespeare survives in his works. A person may be dead, but he continues to make a difference to the world in which he once lived. It is clear, however, that this is purely a figurative use of the word 'survival'. However much it may mean to those who remain after a man has died, it means nothing at all to the man himself once his heart has stopped beating.

The second way in which many people talk and think of survival, but which is excluded by our definition, is, however, worth looking at a little more closely. It is the idea that at death we are, as the phrase commonly goes, 'absorbed into the Infinite', in a way which extinguishes individual awareness in a great continuum of Being. This idea, which owes something to concepts stemming from Eastern religions, is especially attractive to those people who find life so demanding and such a drain on their energies that they like to think of themselves slipping after death into a state in which their life and desires and thoughts and memories are lost in the great Sea of Being—a Sea which is the source of such individualised lives as spring from it for a temporal period, but into which the separate lives sink once more, to be merged in the amorphous mass, when their time is done.

Whether or not these speculations answer to any reality (and personally I believe it is hard to attach much meaning to them), it cannot be said that they support an idea of 'survival after death'. On our definition, the John Jones who survives has to remain conscious that he is the same John Jones who lived in Aberystwyth in 1945, and has to continue to have mental experiences which he can say are John Jones's. Unless John Jones knows that he has survived and that he is still John Jones despite the traumatic experience through which he has gone, no meaning can be given to the word 'survival'.

Admittedly, on this earth it is possible to have a severe accident or a mental breakdown, so that this continuity of self-consciousness is completely lost. A man may suffer from amnesia so that he cannot recall anything to link him with the person he was before his accident or illness. There is only one way in which we can meaningfully speak of him as being the same person after as before, or as having 'survived' his accident or breakdown. That is by reference to his physical brain and body, which remain the same despite the other changes which have come over him. If, however, instead of an accident or breakdown, one speaks of death, it is precisely the physical brain and body which do *not* survive. When there is no continuity of memory and no consciousness of being the same person both sides of the divide, it is not meaningful to talk of 'survival'.

To this argument, some people will reply by reasoning along the following lines: The man who has amnesia is known to be the same person because he is composed of the same bodily tissues. The person who survives death but is absorbed into the Infinite so that he no longer has any knowledge of himself as an individual with individual memories, *has* survived; what remains the same before and after death is the 'soul-stuff' which, so to speak, returns to the pool after death. It is possible to survive an accident without being aware of having done so; it is similarly possible, on this line of argument, to survive death without retaining consciousness.

To this there are two objections. The first is that if after death one is to be as unconscious of the fate of one's 'soul-stuff' as of one's body-stuff, the question of survival loses all its interest. The other is that it is doubtful whether one can legitimately talk of 'soul-stuff' at all, and certain that one cannot meaningfully talk of it as existing without consciousness. Few if any present-day philosophers would concede that what previous generations spoke of as the 'soul' has any existence as an entity in itself. It is simply a shorthand term for that complex of experiences, memories and—in particular—dispositions which the individual builds up during his life. This complex may disintegrate. We observe it in process of disintegration in the more distressing cases of senile decay, and some psychical researchers claim that what they contact is not a complete person who has survived death, but a consciousness in the process of disintegration. If they are right, survival is not a matter of moving from time into eternity, but rather a matter of resisting this disintegration for a specific and limited time after one's physical death. The difficulties and fragmentariness of mediumistic communications are sometimes explained in terms of their being messages from a disintegrated fragment of consciousness; so also are poltergeist phenomena which seem so childish and unintelligent. To that (and the difficulties which the concept raises) we shall be returning in the next chapter. For the moment, we wish only to stress that 'survival' need not mean the permanent survival of the whole consciousness; but that to speak of 'soul-stuff' as though it could be completely distinct from consciouness is to play with meaningless words.

We come back, therefore, to a slightly modified version of our first definition. Survival must involve at least *some* continuity of self-awareness for at least *some* period after the moment of death. What we wish to ask in this present chapter is whether we can argue *a priori* that self-awareness can so survive.

Our arguments can be naïve or sophisticated. Perhaps the simplest philosophy is to say that death is very much like sleep. A man who has died peacefully looks very much like a sleeper. In neither case is it possible to contact the person or to have any communication with him. Yet we know from our own experience that because a man is asleep, it does not mean that he has ceased to have experiences, or that he is not aware that they are experiences of the same man who was awake and is now asleep. Admittedly there are some very strange metamorphoses of surroundings and strange differences in the position from which the surroundings appear to be observed. On waking, perhaps the strangest fact about them is that they did not appear to be strange at the time; but this only shows that the dream world is not the physical world. It remains true that a person who is not in contact with, or contactable by, the outside world can yet have experiences and know that it is he who is having them. If this is true of sleep on this earth, the argument goes, may it not also be true of 'the sleep of death'?

It is an argument (or an analogy) with a long and distinguished history. It is the argument alike of John Donne's sonnet *Death, be not proud,* with its claim that

> From rest and sleepe, which but thy pictures bee,
> Much pleasure, then from thee, much more must flow,

and of Hamlet with his remark 'To die, to sleep; To sleep: perchance to dream.' Its ancestry goes much further back than that. St Paul used it when in 1 Cor. 15.20 he spoke of Christ as 'the first fruits of them that slept' or, in 1 Thess. 4.14, of 'them

... which sleep in Jesus';[1] whilst all four evangelists agree in attributing the usage to Jesus (see Matt. 9.24; Mark 5.39; Luke 8.52; John 11.11). In the Old Testament we find the Book of Daniel (12.2) speaking of the resurrection by claiming that 'many of those who sleep in the dust of the earth will wake', and the traditional description of death, occurring particularly in the books of Kings and Chronicles,[2] is 'he slept with his fathers'.

The antiquity of the idea should not blind us to its inherent difficulties. As a figure of speech it is suggestive and poetic, but as an argument it is distinctly weak. The real difficulty in converting analogy into argument is that of saying why a dreaming man has experiences. Dreams come because the body gives stimuli to the brain; because of the distant note of a bell, or because of the losing battle the stomach is having with the remains of the supper, or because the bedclothes are insecure or the air too oppressive or the body cramped. We know that worry or unfulfilled desire is a prime breeder of dreams, or that a person floating in a saline bath and denied all physical stimuli begins to have hallucinations, but these can be linked with the physical and hormonal secretions connected with the emotions of worry, frustration, or panic. Admittedly, the mind has an astonishingly fecund power of weaving the most complicated fantasy out of apparently unpromising stimuli; but it remains true that all the evidence we have points to the conclusion that if there are no physical (external or hormonal) bodily stimuli, sleep is dreamless. And if you wish to compare death, in which—*ex hypothesi*—the body gives no messages to whatever it is which might survive, with dreamless sleep, you may well be right; but your comparison would not have anything to do with survival. The only characteristic of dreamless sleep is unconsciousness, and we have already pointed out that there is no meaning to survival if we are not conscious of surviving.[3] It seems therefore that the sleep/death parallel is a poetic metaphor which cannot do duty for real argument.

There are subtler forms of the philosophical method. At least since the time of Socrates (who died in 399 BC) it has been common to argue that the brain, which is a part of the body, is separable from the mind or soul, which is independent of it. Soul and body belong to different worlds. Life holds them together in an uneasy harness, but death, the supreme liberator, can be welcomed since it allows them to do what is natural and go their separate ways. So we find Socrates[4] saying, 'when death attacks a man, the mortal portion of him may be supposed to die, but the immortal retires at the approach of death and is preserved safe and indestructible'. What happens to the body is of no concern to the soul. The soul no more depends for its continuing existence on the body than the symphony depends on the particular instruments which are gathered together to play it on one particular evening. The orchestra may be disbanded but the symphony exists for ever, and it can quite easily be re-embodied by bringing together a different set of instruments to play it. Because of his belief in the essential duality of soul and body, Socrates can welcome the hemlock he is offered. Its function is to liberate the essential self, the real or true Socrates, from the body with which that self has been temporarily and fortuitously associated during its earthly life.

This argument has appeal, but what we now know of brain physiology does not give it unqualified support. What happens to our body affects our soul; what happens to our digestion affects our temper; what happens to our brains affects our minds. A zestful and carefree person can be involved in a car accident which leaves him with severe head injuries, and when he is physically recovered, he has become moody and lethargic, and has no memory whatever of the time before his car went into the skid. When the brain grows old and tired, and senile decay attacks its bodily cells, the personality changes. If the brain cells are starved of oxygen, mental effort becomes harder and harder. The content and quality of our consciousness depends so closely upon the state (and in particular on the chemical environment) of the brain cells that it is hard to believe that it is not the brain which determines it all. It is easier to believe that when our body decays and the brain cells decay with it, our consciousness evaporates.

On the other hand, whilst it is certain that the brain and consciousness are closely related, we need to ask what *kind* of relation there is between the two. Is it (to use the terms employed in the nineteenth century by William James) a productive or a transmissive relation? Is the brain a generator which produces consciousness or an instrument through which consciousness operates? On the former view (the view argued in the preceding paragraph), it is akin to a television transmitter; on the latter, to a television set. You cannot see a television picture without a television set, and even if you have one, you will find that throwing a hammer at the screen is a very effective way of making the programme disappear; but such drastic action does not destroy the programme. The show exists independently of the set, and all that the hammer has destroyed is the delicately adjusted instrument which enables it to be perceived. When your set breaks down, you are cut off from the show in the studio, but the show still goes on. Similarly, if you destroy the brain, you do not thereby destroy the personality; you only make it impossible for the independently existing personality to express itself physically in this present world. If the brain is injured, the mind is isolated, not annihilated. Old age and senility are not signs of the disintegration of the mind but the breakdown of the instrument whereby the mind is expressed in consciousness and whereby it communicates with other embodied consciousnesses.

An example comes to mind. I was told some while ago by one of the technicians at Stoke Mandeville hospital of a young girl with gradually spreading paralysis. She was propped up motionless in bed, her head held in place by a looped bandage tied to the bed-head. She was blind; she was fed by a tube in her neck; she could only breathe because a machine was constantly pumping air into and out of her lungs. The only physical movement of which she was capable was a slight twitch in one toe. To the outsider, here was a case of purely vegetative existence, a repulsive hulk of a body which it would be better to let die, a brain and a mind which had ceased to function. Yet through the miracles of electronic engineering and a device known as the Patient-Operated Selector Mechanism ('Possum') that twitch of the toe could operate an electric typewriter through which the girl could carry on a conversation and write poetry. The brain had virtually ceased to carry out its motor functions, but the mind was as active as ever.

Another form of the same argument depends on the fact that our bodies—and this includes our brains—are constantly being renewed. No physical particle of which my brain is composed today is identical with any particle of which it was composed (say) seven years ago; yet I am the same person now as then and (despite grey hairs and wrinkles) recognisably the same size and shape. What is it which makes a man the same person despite all the fluctuations and changes that occur in the matter of which his physical frame is composed? What is it which holds the personality together? There must be something which remains a constant in the changing flux of our mortal bodies, so that we are the same person today as ten, twenty, thirty years ago. This something is apart from the body; may it not be separable and separate so that when our bodies run to dust, this organising principle remains as the core and ground of a personality which can subsist without a body on which to operate?

It is doubtful whether this argument can stand the weight of the case. It might be more easily sustained if, like the snake shedding its winter coat, the immortal part of man could be observed during a person's life sloughing away one physical body and assuming an entirely different one to serve it for the next seven-year period; but the seven-year change is a gradual one, and it depends entirely on there being sufficient of the old unchanged body left to allow new cells to grow in a place and form identical with that of the discarded ones. We know increasingly more nowadays about the biochemical reasons why cells reproduce and still retain their form and characteristics, and why—when they decay—they are replaced by new cells having the same pattern and arrangement as the old ones. If we hold on to this argument, our reasoning will soon be overtaken by physiological research, and the soul as organising principle of the body will turn out to be nothing more spiritual than the genetic code in a double helix of carbon chains with a unique pattern of amino-acids sticking out of it.

The trouble with all arguments of this sort is that they are an easy prey to those philosophers who tell us that we cannot speak of mind and matter as though they were two distinct entities which can have relations of association or separation. They point out to us that when matter has reached a high enough degree of complexity of form and organisation of structure, it may become self-replicating and we meet with the phenomenon called 'life'. At a very much higher level of structure and organisation, life can be expressed in a brain, and at a higher level still, this brain can become capable of self-awareness. 'Mind' is simply a shorthand term for 'those states of self-consciousness which are empirically observed in beings of a certain complexity of brain organisation'—that is, as known to us, only in *homo sapiens*. Rudiments of it are present in the higher primates, but their complexity of neurophysiological organisation is not enough to do much in this way. There is a single entity which is a 'self-conscious human being'. We can look at this entity in two different ways, the mental and the neurophysiological. Dualism—the talk about 'mind' and 'matter' as separable— is an unreflective way of making two entities out of two aspects of an indivisible unity. We know (and *can* know) nothing of mental states causally unconnected with neurophysiological happenings and it is gratuitous to suppose that the two can be separated.

Whether this be true or not, the certainty for which we have been looking seems to be slipping away from us. Let us move, therefore, from philosophical arguments to moral ones. We may talk of the mocking sense of limited achievement that flaunts itself in the face of our limited span on earth. We may talk of the sense of incompletion which attends our work on earth.[5] But we still find no firm *locus standi* along these lines. They cannot be held to show us anything about the structure of the universe. 'If only . . .', we may say; but our very 'if only . . .' shows that we are hoping and longing for what cannot be. Belief in survival arose, according to Bertrand Russell, 'as an emotional reaction to the fear of death', and, he warns us, 'We have no right to expect the universe to adapt itself to our emotions.'[6] The moral argument from our innate sense of justice is equally unconvincing. It *is* unjust that the righteous should suffer and the unrepentant blackguard die peacefully in his bed at the age of eighty-five, but that by itself is no argument for immortality. Perhaps the universe *is* one vast mocking or meaningless system against which the wits and the rationality and the sense of justice of man are idiot's tales of no significance.

It looks, therefore, as if the arguments of pure, unaided reason are two-edged. Some people may be more convinced by one side of the discussions we have just outlined than by the other, but it cannot be denied that neither side has made out an incontrovertible case. If we are looking for certainty, we have not yet found a sound enough basis for it.

3   Psychic phenomena

IT will be the contention of this chapter that psychical research provides us with ample data relevant to the question of whether men survive death.[1] They may be divided into occurrences which happen unsought and experiments which are more consciously contrived. Both types of evidence seem compelling at first sight; the case begins to crumble when examined in the light of alternative explanations, though it can to some extent be reinstated by a subtler approach to the question.

If the dead survive, how might we expect them to make contact with us? The most obvious and (to the unsophisticated observer) the most convincing way would be by appearing to us and conversing with us. This does not mean that the dead person would need to take to himself a physical body in order to stand in the same room as a living person who sees him, nor that he needs to have physical vocal chords or lips in order for the living person to hear him speaking. After all, quite apart from psychic phenomena, we know that it is possible to see or hear what is not there. Not only is there imagination—

> Such tricks hath strong imagination,
> That, if it would but apprehend some joy,
> It comprehends some bringer of that joy;
> Or in the night, imagining some fear,
> How easy is a bush suppos'd a bear![2]

—and the will to believe; there are also hallucinations caused by hypnosis or drugs. It is therefore quite possible to suppose that a deceased communicator could stimulate the optic nerve or act directly on the appropriate brain cells in order to give to the living person sensations which are identical with those he would have if the deceased person were physically present in the room with him. That, incidentally, disposes of the old chestnut about its being easy to suppose that there could be the ghost of a person, but to believe that there could be ghosts of his clothes is another matter.

But has such a thing ever happened? And, if it has, how can we know that the true explanation was not in such mundane terms as imagination or the will to believe? The question becomes even more embarrassing when we allow that the departed may find it easier to communicate with us in our dreams than in our waking moments. Visual apparitions are pretty startling and unusual happenings; dreams are the common property of us all, and their explanation in terms of psychology or digestion is well known.

Two factors in particular might give us reason to pause before accepting the sceptic's explanation. One would be if the person who had the experience was at the time unaware of the death of the person whom he saw or heard. The other would be if what he saw or heard conveyed information known to the departed person but not to the living.

This discussion is getting too abstract. Let us look at some actual cases in which the first and most unsophisticated explanation is that a dead person has communicated with a living one before the fact of his death was known, or that he has given the living person information he could have got from no one else but the departed.

In April 1968 I received a letter from Sir Fred Pritchard from which he has allowed me to quote the following extract:

My father was a fruit merchant of Liverpool and I am a retired High Court Judge: so that our joint background should not be such as to suggest unduly imaginative qualities. My father in his earlier years used to travel on business every year to America and had a seafaring brother whom he called 'Chink'. On the occasion of the story my father, returning by steamship from America and in mid-Atlantic, was about to go to bed when he heard the latch of his cabin door click and looking up saw his brother, he used to say so clearly that he actually spoke the words 'Hello—Chink!'.

On his arrival at Liverpool he received the news that on the day of this occurrence his brother had died of yellow fever in the Canary Islands.

Communication may, of course, be by voice alone, without an accompanying vision. The next case happened to a retired clergyman on 11 March 1965 and was given to the Society for Psychical Research about three months later.

> At about half past 12 on that day I sat down to breakfast/lunch in my dining-room no one else being in the room or my house and having said my Grace, a thing I do not always do, I heard a clear male voice saying distinctly 'I AM HERE', the voice very much resembling that of my nephew Charles B. . . . I made a note of this strange occurrence later on in the day in my diary but it was not until I turned to look at my *Daily Telegraph* and there saw with a shock of surprise and I may say of grief that they were writing his obituary and that he was dead.[3]

In neither of these cases was any information passed on to the person who saw or heard. Even the fact that 'Chink' Pritchard or Charles B. was dead had to be discovered subsequently and through normal channels. What makes these cases suggestive is the time-coincidence and the fact that the persons 'seen' or 'heard' were not at the time known to be dead. Had they happened to the same percipients a fortnight later, the experience would have been disturbing, but a normal explanation would be preferred to a paranormal one.[4]

Unless, that is, the apparition had passed on some information which the dead person knew but the living did not. In the following case, that is precisely what happened. Mr Lucian Landau writes:

> Mr Constantin Antoniadés is a friend of mine. . . . We met to discuss business in a West End hotel on 4 November 1955. I noticed that he was very upset and he told me that he had recently lost his wife under tragic circumstances. . . .
>
> On 5 December I went to Geneva to visit him on business. . . . In the evening he took me to stay with himself

and his sister at his home. . . . I was asleep almost as soon as my head touched the pillow.

I woke up suddenly with the feeling that someone had entered my room. I had been sleeping on my right side with my face to the wall. I turned over and saw what I can only describe as a pool of faint light. It was elliptical in shape, with its longer axis vertical, and did not have a sharp outline. I noticed that, although it appeared as light to me, it did not illuminate any of the objects in the room, which was in pitch darkness. Within the lighted area I saw the figure of a lady whom I recognized as my host's deceased wife. She seemed to smile. Next to her stood an Alsatian dog. His coat was brown, not the usual sable and black. I thought I heard a whisper, 'Tell him.' Then it all disappeared. The room was black. The house was silent. My luminous watch indicated 4.20 a.m. I was wide awake and it was some time before I fell asleep again.

At breakfast I asked Mr Antoniadés whether his wife had had an all-brown Alsatian dog. 'Oh, yes,' he replied, 'he is still alive.' I expressed my surprise as I could see no sign of any animal in the house, and he explained, 'No, the dog is not here. When my wife became ill I found it difficult to look after him and I had to give him away. He is in some kennels some sixty miles away from here.'[5]

At Mr Landau's insistence, Mr Antoniadés later rang the kennels to inquire about the dog, to be told that it had been destroyed a few days before. All-brown Alsatians are very rare dogs, which makes the explanation by coincidence that much less likely.

Cases in which a vision or dream of a dead person has given information unknown to the living person who has the vision have been known for centuries. For example, St Augustine of Hippo told of this incident sixteen hundred years ago:

In Milan a man was called upon to pay a large debt which his father, who had died a short time previously, had contracted. To his son's great dismay the creditor presented the father's I.O.U. which was found correct and not tampered with. The son, however, who had never heard a

word about this debt, could not find the receipt proving that
the debt had been paid.

In his great trouble this man one night had a dream in
which his father appeared to him and indicated the place
where the receipt could be found, as the debt had indeed
been paid off completely. And so the son could prove the
debt paid and the creditor a swindler.[6]

Now (as we have already hinted) there is such a thing as
coincidence; and the cases we have so far given may simply be
examples of a very small number of coincidences which have
happened over the years. When we consider the number of
dreams which have *not* led to the discovery of lost receipts, the
number of visions which have *not* been corroborated by the
information that the person seen in the vision did in fact own
the particular kind of rare dog with which she was seen, and
the number of apparitions which have *not* afterwards been
found to coincide with the death of the person seen, the
apparently startling cases present us with a less than watertight case for survival. Two pieces of extensive statistical
research, however (one classical and the other more recent),
show us that coincidence needs to be a surprisingly far-fetched
hypothesis.

The classical research project was the 'Census of
Hallucinations' carried out by the Society for Psychical
Research in 1889–94. This question was asked:

> Have you ever, when believing yourself to be completely
> awake, had a vivid impression of seeing or being touched by
> a living being or inanimate object, or of hearing a voice;
> which impression, so far as you could discover, was not due
> to any external physical cause?

Seventeen thousand replies were received, and 1300 of these
answers were in the affirmative. Of these, sixty-five concerned
apparitions of persons seen within twelve hours before or after
their death. Stringent tests of the quality and value of the
reported accounts were able to cut down this number to an
irreducible bedrock of thirty-two evidentially sound cases. At
that time the probability that any one person taken at random

would die on a given day was about 1 in 19,000. If, therefore, these cases of apparitions occurring in connection with a death were pure coincidence, and if it was as likely that an apparition would be seen on any other day than the day of death, one would expect that 1 in 19,000 of those 1300 reported apparitions would be of persons who had died within twelve hours either way of being seen. The reported number of thirty-two cases is 440 times the statistical expectation on the hypothesis of chance coincidence.[7] The figures show us that the long arm of coincidence is not nearly long enough to account for the frequency of cases.

Unfortunately, however, the case is not so simply proved as that, and a great deal of cold water has subsequently been poured upon this nineteenth-century research project.

It had methodological defects. For example, the 17,000 answers did not come from a statistically random selection of the population, and it is more likely that people with stories to tell like that of Sir Fred Pritchard should tell them than that the records should be swollen by 'nil returns' or by accounts of apparently unmotivated or meaningless paranormal experiences. In any case, *can* evidence of this kind prove anything about survival of death? Those striking cases in which an apparition was seen within hours (or even minutes) of the distant friend's death could have been the result of a last desperate telepathic message from the expiring mind. The fact that the figure was *seen* after the death of the 'agent' might only mean that the information had lain latent in the mind of the percipient for those few crucial hours. The most we could hope to prove would be the reality of telepathy between the living. The cases are suggestive, but not conclusive.

Similar arguments could be deployed on those cases where unknown information was passed on. The cynic could claim that it was known to *some* living person at the time, even if he had forgotten that he knew it. For example, we could argue that Mr Antoniadés, who knew all about his wife's dog, was responsible for subconsciously passing on a telepathic message about it to Mr Landau. The latter in his turn allowed his dreaming self to dress up the information in such a way as to suggest it came from the deceased Mrs Antoniadés.

As we suggested at the beginning of the chapter, the case for survival is beginning to crumble. Can a more sophisticated approach rescue it?

The sophistication is provided by a research project carried out by Professor Hornell Hart and his collaborators in the 1950s.[8] His team reviewed six theories of the nature of apparitions in the light of a careful statistical analysis of 165 cases. Of each apparition they asked a large number of questions such as 'Did it look "solid" or "real"?', 'Was it seen by more than one person at the same time?', 'Did it appear or disappear suddenly or inexplicably?', 'Was it seen by a person with whom the appearer had some strong bond of relationship or friendship?' The apparitions were then divided into groups, and each group then had a 'fingerprint' which consisted of the percentage of cases in which the answer to each individual question was 'Yes'. (For example, in the case of that group out of the total of 165 which consisted of apparitions of the dead or dying, the percentages answering 'yes' to the four questions above was 23, 10, 38 and 78.) The larger the number of questions asked, the more detailed the 'fingerprint'. For their main analysis, Professor Hart's group chose a 23-point fingerprint. If, now, two different groups of cases possess the same 'fingerprint', it is to be presumed that they are identically caused. The techniques of statistical mathematics have to be applied to the results to see whether the differences between fingerprints are such as would be expected by pure chance or whether they indicate that the two groups are essentially different.

The first important result was obtained by dividing the cases into two groups, of high and low 'evidentiality'. Each case was given an 'evidentiality rating', varying from 0·01 to 0·90, according to whether there was independent corroboration; whether the report had been committed to writing before confirmation of the evidential details had been received; how long had elapsed between the occurrence and its committal to writing; and so forth. What was expected was that the two groups would have been quite different, because there had been greater opportunity in the 'low-evidentiality' cases to embellish the accounts with what Pooh-Bah might have called 'corroborative detail, intended to give artistic verisimilitude to an otherwise bald and unconvincing narrative'. In fact, the difference in the fingerprints of the high and low cases was found to be 'practically negligible'. We can therefore use the whole collection of 165 cases in the knowledge that, although some of them are better evidenced than others, this fact does not interfere with their fingerprint details.

With this point secured, Hart and his team divided the cases into five classes:

1. Apparitions of those dead twelve hours or longer.
2. Apparitions of those dead up to twelve hours.
3. Apparitions seen at the moment of death.
4. Apparitions of living persons, in which the person who was seen retained some memory of what had happened during the apparition.
5. Apparitions of living persons who were unaware of having appeared to anyone at the time.

The fourth class—conscious apparitions of the living—needs some explanation, which can best be given by quoting an actual case.[9] Mr Jensen, a publisher of Copenhagen, was away from home in Randers. His wife had never been in that town. One night she was woken up by a thunderstorm and had an intense desire to contact her husband. Suddenly she had a vision of him going along an alley and entering a house. She watched him go up to his room and undress and was annoyed because he did not use the ointment she had got for his face. The next day she wrote to him at the office, telling him what had happened. That very night, in his hotel, after a walk down an alley-way, he had gone to bed. During the night he woke to see the figure of his wife standing beside the bed. Her description of the alley and the hotel was 'entirely adequate' both to the house and its surroundings. In other words, the person whose apparition was seen (Mrs Jensen) retained conscious memory of what happened whilst her apparition was being perceived by her husband. Had she been unaware of this, the case would have gone into class 5 above, rather than into class 4.

The conclusion to which Professor Hart was compelled by a

statistical examination of the differences between the five classes into which he divided the cases, was that apparitions of the dead are basically similar in character to conscious apparitions of the living—at least in most of the twenty-three particulars for which he carried out his statistical analysis. He goes on to draw out the consequences of this similarity:

> Apparitions of the dead, like these conscious apparitions of the living, may be vehicles within which the conscious personalities of the individual represented go on with their past loves, hopes, and interests, carrying with them memories of the past, and purposes for the future, and using these apparitions as vehicles for observation and operation. In a word, this comparison would seem to strengthen the hypothesis of the survival of personality beyond bodily death. . . .
>
> Indeed, of the 25 cases of conscious apparitions of the living, 22 involved either special concern for loved ones, or dreaming about the percipient, or some other direction of attention towards the percipient by the appearer. This may be highly important. If apparitions of the dead and the dying are essentially the same sort of phenomenon as are conscious apparitions of the living, and if conscious apparitions of the living involve almost always a definite direction of attention by the appearer towards the percipient, does this not strengthen the hypothesis that apparitions of the dead do frequently involve actual directions of attention by surviving personalities towards the loved ones who perceive their apparitions?[10]

That last question was phrased with commendably academic caution. By the nature of the case, we cannot ask the deceased person whose apparition was seen whether he was conscious of his continued existence and whether, if so, he was aware that he was appearing to an earthly friend; but Professor Hart has shown that the apparition of the dead person is so like that of the living person of whom such a question can be asked (and to which the answer is often in the affirmative) that it is at least *prima facie* likely that the answer would be the same.

But we are still far from *proof*. The sophisticated techniques of Professor Hart have not *compelled* the sceptic to withdraw, even if they have drawn some of the sting of his contentions. It is time to see whether the same holds true of the other kind of evidence—that of the contrived experiment as contrasted with the unsought and spontaneous case. This will lead us to examine the claims of mediumship.

Mediums (or as they may with less begging of questions be called, 'sensitives') claim that they can in certain circumstances be used to convey messages from discarnate entities. Most mediums believe they are in contact with a small number of 'controls', who use the body of the medium to pass on messages they have received from a much larger number of departed people, to the 'sitters' who have asked the sensitive to act on their behalf. Contact therefore is generally made through a chain: communicator–control–sensitive–sitter. Occasionally (in the case of some mediums, regularly) the control will, as it were, step aside and allow the communicator to express himself directly to the sitter through the sensitive. Some sensitives prefer to deal only with a small circle of communicators without the intervention of controls.

The control can operate either verbally through the vocal chords of the medium, or in writing. In the latter case, the medium holds a pen or pencil lightly in her hand[11] and makes no conscious attempt to move it over the page. Eventually it moves of its own accord. At first it is hard to get more than scribble, and when words appear, they may at first be no more than gibberish. But with perseverance, the medium can train the faculty of 'automatic writing' so that the messages which appear make sense. The use of devices such as the ouija board or of table-rapping is generally left to the amateur motivated by curiosity, and is emphatically not to be recommended.[12]

Mediumship itself is a very varied thing. Some is exercised in no more than a state of relaxation; some in a trance so deep that the medium herself has no knowledge afterwards of what was said and done during the sitting. Some mediums ply for hire, others are amateurs. Some have deliberately developed their powers; others have found that the powers manifest themselves unbidden, and they exercise them reluctantly.

Equally varied are the answers which can be given to the question 'are mediums genuine?' Undoubtedly some are knowing frauds. There are others whose performances satisfy themselves and their clients, but who, to unbiased investigators, seem singularly uninspired. Others again, though women of integrity, are discovered to be quite unconsciously dressing up material which they have received normally and presenting it as of paranormal origin. Mediumship is usually exercised in a state of mental dissociation, when subconscious forces have the greatest chance of affecting what the sensitive says or does.

The sitter, too, needs to have his critical wits about him. It is necessary, for instance, to match a list of statements made by a medium to one sitter with a second list made to an entirely different sitter. Only if the first sitter gives a consistently higher score of hits on his own script than he gives to the control list which was not supposed to refer to him (and of which he does not know that it does not refer to him), can we begin to suspect that anything more than the will to believe is the true explanation of the medium's success. Even then, we are not out of the wood. Has the medium been fishing for clues, either in the sitter's replies to her questions, or by his facial expressions when, after a series of 'sighting shots', the medium begins to get 'warm'? The unsophisticated sitter can very readily indeed be taken in.[13]

There are cases, however, where all the tests seem to indicate that the dross has been eliminated and we are left with pure gold—that rare sensitive who has been proved not to be even unconsciously cheating, and whose statements hit the target with uncanny accuracy. Have we here got the proof for which we have long been looking? Is this our assurance of genuine communication with the departed? Unfortunately, no. Once more, we find that there are other ways of interpreting the evidence.

Suppose a sensitive tells me things about my deceased great-aunt Ada which strike me as far more apposite to the real great-aunt than a similar series of statements by the same sensitive about somebody else's great-aunt. I still need not assume that the sensitive is really in touch with Aunty, who is alive and well and living in the spirit world. After all, there am I, sitting in front of the medium, and I know far more than she ever will of my great-aunt and her peculiarities. Why should not the sensitive have telepathically tapped my memories of the old lady and dressed them up as post-mortem messages?

Even if I try to get round this by not being present at the sitting myself, but by asking someone else to sit as my proxy, we know that telepathy is notoriously unaffected by distance and that there is no need for me to be consciously thinking of a subject in order for my unconscious memories to be available for telepathic tapping. Or suppose I am told things about the old lady which I never knew before. If I cannot check them, their value as evidence is nil; but if I can check them, and do so, they then become part of my mental possessions, so that (in theory at any rate) the medium could acquire the necessary information by precognition of what I was going to discover. Or the whole thing could be a case of clairvoyance, in which the medium becomes paranormally aware of the whereabouts or nature of a physical object without the intervention of any human mind, either incarnate or discarnate. Any one of these explanations—singly or together—could drive a coach and six through the attempt to interpret mediumship as involving contact with the surviving departed.

For example, here is an instance of what are known as 'book tests', used extensively by the medium Mrs Leonard. Her control was called 'Feda' and the sitters on this occasion were Lord Glenconner and his son. The communicator was Wyndham ('Bim') Tennant, another son of Lord Glenconner, who had been killed in the First World War. Lord Glenconner was keen on forestry and, in the course of family walks through the woods, would gloomily say that the young trees were being ruined by 'the beetle'. Young Bim had been known to whisper to his mother at the start of such a walk, 'See if we can get through the wood without hearing about the beetle.' At the sitting in question Feda, through Mrs Leonard, said the following:

Bim now wants to send a message to his father. *This book is particularly for his father;* underline that, he says. It is the ninth book on the third shelf counting from left to right in the bookcase on the right of the door in the drawing room. Take the title, and through it page thirty-seven.

The book indicated was *Trees*. The sentence running from page 36 through to page 37 read:

Sometimes you will see curious marks in the wood; these are caused by a tunnelling beetle, very injurious to the trees.[14]

What are we to make of this? Was the truth less dramatic and has memory written it up more convincingly? Was it a coincidence in that many pages of many books in Lord Glenconner's drawing room might have conjured up memories of his son? Was it telepathy with the sitters? Was it precognition of the confirmatory examination of the book? Or had Bim chosen this test because it was the best way to convince his father that it was really he who was communicating? (And if so, how can the departed spirits know what is written on the pages of closed books on earth?) We do not have to complain that the explanations not involving survival are far-fetched, for it is the contention of those who are unconvinced of survival that *any* explanation is less far-fetched than the explanation that the dead survive and can still refer to books in their fathers' libraries. If that attitude is taken, then obviously any loophole is big enough to wriggle through.

Be that as it may, we see that the evidence of mediumship is proving a broken reed. Unless we can employ it more subtly, we cannot use it to prove survival.

The 'cross-correspondences' may provide the answer. They were the work of a group of sensitives in the period from about 1906 to about 1930, including Mrs Verrall (a Cambridge don) and her daughter Helen; Mrs Fleming, the sister of Rudyard Kipling; Dame Edith Lyttelton; and Mrs Coombe-Tennant, a senior civil servant. (The last three used the pseudonyms Mrs Holland, Mrs King, and Mrs Willett.) The communicators included three of the founders of the SPR, Frederic Myers, Edmund Gurney, and Henry Sidgwick, joined later by Dr

Verrall and Henry Butcher. All these died between 1888 and 1912.

The various sensitives produced automatic writing, and it began to be noticed that there were references in the script of one automatist to material which appeared in the script of another. In the end the automatists were isolated so that they never read each others' scripts; yet the colossal jigsaw, spread over thousands of scripts written over about a quarter of a century, continued unabated. It began to look as if there was a communicating intelligence or intelligences which, instead of giving a message in a single script, distributed it amongst several, dropping clues in each so that the links could be followed up. Moreover, the ostensible communicators were distinguished classical scholars, though few of the sensitives had much knowledge of the classics. Recondite classical allusions could therefore be made without the automatists' realising what the scripts were up to; and the fact that such allusions were made would strengthen the case for seeing it as the work of the communicators and not of the sensitives.

Moreover, the communicators were not content simply to *prove* their existence. They thought they could work for the benefit of the inhabitants of this earth, even though they had left it behind. Thus the cross-correspondences indicate a great plan which

> sets out a scheme for the creation of a peaceful world-order, of which the Pax Romana is an imperfect archetype, to be promoted by a great body of discarnate intelligences, of which seven specified Communicators are members and prophets, and to be achieved by the creation of a race of 'children of the spirit'.[15]

This may sound over-drawn and almost risible to the present generation, but it rings true to the idealism of Myers and his associates.

To examine the simplest of cross-correspondences here would take up a disproportionate amount of space. All we can do is to give some estimate of their significance.[16] In the opinion of W.H. Salter :

the scheme is really there, and not an invention of the perfervid ingenuity of the interpreters, for it rests on careful documentation, painstaking research into facts, and commonsense handling of symbols and allusions. The intricacy combined with consistency of the scheme shows that it was not fortuitous. Common association of ideas among the automatists, and the spread of knowledge of each others' scripts through publication in the *Proceedings* of the Society, and through correspondence and conversation between them, are doubtless contributing factors, but inadequate as an explanation of the whole affair. They do not account for paranormal references appearing independently in the scripts of several members. Incidentally the spread of information by normal means was never uncontrolled nor unrecorded, and allowance for it was made when the scripts came to be interpreted. In default of any sufficiently normal explanation, a paranormal one must be sought.[15]

In other words, those who have studied the matter most carefully believe we shall get closer to certainty through an examination of the cross-correspondences than in any other way. Nevertheless, some doubt remains, for it has always to be asked whether the investigators in their enthusiasm have not discovered clues and linkages between the scripts which exist only in their imagination, or whether one or other of the automatists may not have been 'directing' the operation unwittingly and telepathically. Let the last, judicial, word on the cross-correspondences be that of Chancellor Garth Moore, clergyman, barrister-at-law, and student of psychical research:

Psychical Research alone has not incontrovertibly established survival, for so often telepathy and precognition provide logically possible alternative explanations. But, on a balance of probability, these alternatives should often be rejected as too far-fetched to be economical; and this is especially true in the instances of cross-correspondence.[17]

We have looked at spontaneous apparitions and the communications received by sensitives. There is one final type of material which must be mentioned and that is the experience of being 'out of the body'.[18] Let me give an example:

> During the war in the Western Desert, I was knocked unconscious by bomb blast and had the peculiar sensation of being out of my body viewing the scene from a point about 20 feet above the ground. . . . I could hear the aircraft as it came in on another attack and the voices of my companions. I could see the dust clearing away from the explosion that had knocked me unconscious and my own body lying there on the gravel.[19]

This weird experience of seeing one's body from outside can be initiated in a number of ways. Severe shock (as in the case above) is one; another is extreme illness. Dr George Ritchie, a psychiatrist, tells of how—in his army medical school days in 1943—he had a severe bout of 'flu and accidentally took an almost fatal overdose of aspirin. He collapsed and was in a coma for four days. 'His own experience was that, after collapsing, the next thing he knew was that he found himself sitting on the edge of his bed, and surveying with distaste his body on the bed.' He found his uniform, appeared to dress, and began to make his way out of the hospital, but was disturbed to find himself walking through an orderly carrying a tray of instruments. He flew away at tremendous speed to Gettysburg (a town to which he had not previously been, but the features of which he recognised on a later visit); then back to his bed in hospital where his body lay covered in a sheet. His subsequent experiences before regaining consciousness were more of a symbolic, dream, or mystical nature, which could probably be described as 'the product of a very fevered brain'.[20]

Indeed, this might be the explanation of all the cases of this type, were it not for the fact that some of the people who have experienced it are able to 'see' or 'hear' things going on in places apart from their physical bodies, which have afterwards been verified as correct. G. S. Whitby tells of a student of his who was rushed to hospital with a severe internal haemorrhage and whose heart ceased to beat whilst on the operating table. Resuscitation was successful, but during this time of physical death the student 'found herself against the far wall, watching her body on the operating table and seeing and hearing all that went on. When she later told the surgeon, he had to admit that her account was accurate to the last detail.' She had never before seen the hospital, and was in a deep coma on admission. Mr Whitby corroborated the account himself with the surgeon.[21]

This type of experience can happen at other times than when the body is under severe stress, and is a great deal commoner than many people realise.[22] It happens frequently in dreams but also in waking experience. Dr J. H. M. Whiteman, a physicist and mathematician, has kept a meticulous diary over more than thirty years which includes over 2500 entries relating to his experiences. Most of them are visual, and in them he occupies a spiritual 'form' or 'body' in an 'other world' with whose denizens she converses and whose geography she explores. I say 'she' because, curiously, Dr Whiteman's form during these experiences is that of a pre-adolescent girl. He enters what he calls the 'mystical state' either by awakening his consciousness during a dream, or by observing a bright scene in a circular 'opening' in the physical world (for example, in a crystal ball) and going through it.

The range of experiences reported by people in a state like this is astonishingly varied.

> There are all grades of this experience from a mere detachment of the self from the physical body, which is looked down upon from a varying distance, up to an ascent of the self to astral realms of existence where the soul bodies of the deceased are met. . . . But the most exalted, most illumined out-of-the-body experience takes the self into a vast realm of pure light sustained by a love of such magnitude that the whole created universe trembles in blessing in the eternity of its Creator, the Father Almighty.[23]

The fully mystical experience is rare, but the simple sensation of being out of the physical body is by no means uncommon. C. E. Green asked 380 Oxford undergraduates (not randomly selected, but volunteers for experiments in extra-sensory perception) whether they had ever had such an experience; 131 said that they had. A nationwide appeal by Miss Green for accounts of similar experiences resulted in her receiving nearly a thousand cases.[24] It was frequently reported that the centre of consciousness from which the physical body was observed was attached to that body by an extensible cord. This is a phenomenon which often turns up in the literature of out-of-the-body experiences, and number of writers have connected it with the 'silver cord' of Ecclesiastes:

> Remember your Creator . . . before the sun and the light of day give place to darkness, . . . when the guardians of the house tremble, . . . and those who look through the windows look no longer. Remember him before the silver cord is snapped and the golden bowl is broken, before the pitcher is shattered at the spring and the wheel broken at the well, before the dust returns to the earth as it began and the spirit returns to God who gave it. (Eccles. 12.1–7)

In this, they are certainly mistaken. Ecclesiastes is simply using poetic metaphors. The house is the body, the windows the eyes, the golden bowl the skull and the silver cord the spine. Or, if we take it a little more prosaically, the Preacher is using 'figures of death: the ornamental lamp is extinguished when its *cord* is *cut*, and its *bowl* falls and is *broken*'.[25] We see how misleading it can be to mistake a poetic Hebrew metaphor for sober fact. Whether the 'cord' of the astral travellers has any existence or not, it cannot claim biblical support.

That does not, however, absolve us from asking what we are to make of this strange experience of being 'out-of-the-body'. Does it suggest that consciousness is not tied to the physical body, that it can to some extent come loose before death and contact the living and the departed, and that it can therefore reasonably be expected to continue existing quite independently of the body after death? That would be one way in which to read the evidence, but it is by no means the only one. For instance, it is known that when all sensory stimuli are withdrawn from a person, strange things begin to happen to his mental processes. These range from processions of imaginary elephants to convictions of inner truth, and there is no way of telling whether the latter are any more objective than the former. Similarly, Aldous Huxley's celebrated attempts, in *The Doors of Perception* and *Heaven and Hell*, to extract material of permanent and universal significance from the stuff of his visions when under drugs, may tell us more about Huxley than about the Ultimate. May the same not be true of Dr Whiteman? A psychologist would want to interpret his visions in terms of dream-symbolism, and would see the immense amount of intellectual effort which he expended in explaining the nature of his revelation as being no more than the efforts of rationalisation against interpreting their origin as psycho-pathological. His life-story would then be of great interest for giving us insights into the psychology of mysticism, but of no significance in teaching us of the nature of a life in a world to come.

Psychologists and physiologists can be equally sceptical about the commoner experience of being out of the body.

The apparent orientation of one's body in space depends mainly on sensory impressions from the three semi-circular canals within each inner ear. Their influence may readily be demonstrated by pirouetting on one's toes with the head bowed down at different angles and in different directions (on the chest or over one or other shoulder).

Disturbances in any of these sensory cues may induce a temporary feeling that the apparent centre or origin of one's consciousness (usually taken to be a point in the head behind the eyes) has a different situation or orientation from that suggested by sensations from the rest of the body. A change in the blood pressure within the inner ears is especially apt to evoke the experience of rising, hovering, or floating away in space. Such changes are most liable to occur in a recumbent posture. . . . In susceptible individuals they may be precipitated by a rise in temperature, by slight digestive disturbances, or as a result of the automatic reflexes occurring in emotional stress. . . .

Persons with vivid optical imagery habitually visualize their own bodies; and when (as not infrequently happens on critical occasions) the vividness approaches that of an actual sensation, they naturally assume that they have temporarily acquired the position in space from which this visual picture would be obtained.[26]

Or, to put it in more technical language, 'Medical interpretations of these phenomena are usually in terms of the transposition of proprioceptive, and other, sensory inputs into corresponding visual imagery.'[27] In the crisis cases, there are psychological factors involved. The intolerable conditions in which the physical body is existing are escaped by shutting off consciousness of bodily sensations and the resultant detachment is symbolised by a hallucinatory separation from the physical body.

Some people have learnt, as they believe, to step out of the body when its suffering becomes too great to be borne. Madame Julia de Beausobre achieved this during long confinement in the Lubianka prison, and a sober head teacher told me that when a prisoner of war in Japan he too had learnt to do it when things became too bad. He said he had been able to teach most, but not all, of his fellow-prisoners to do the same.[28]

Sometimes the apparent separation seems to be a direct effect, voluntary or involuntary, of a desire to escape from some intolerable predicament. It is a trick, as I can testify from several case-studies, often acquired by children who are unlucky enough to get into constant hot water with their teachers or their school fellows.[29]

When I was being publicly scolded in class I had no difficulty in escaping to a far corner of the ceiling, whence I could look down with amused pity at the poor little boy on the bench below. My visual powers faded in early adolescence.[30]

Finally, the veridical element in these experiences could be interpreted either in terms of telepathy or clairvoyance (which often seems to work most effectively when the normal functioning of the mind is suspended or its normal controls relaxed) or of that kind of hyperacuity of senses which parapsychologists often detect in the less well-controlled experiments in extra-sensory perception. It is well known by priests and doctors that patients who are apparently comatose can hear, understand, and remember what is being said around them far more than their visitors often realise.[31] Words heard in a coma may be translated into an hallucination which, recounted afterwards, may appear to have veridical components.

Once more, the certainty for which we are looking has eluded us. We can interpret the phenomena at which we have been looking either sceptically or with the will to believe, but we cannot compel others to accept our interpretation—either way.

And, finally, what could we expect to prove by the methods of psychical research? That 'the personality of man'[32] is a more complex and mysterious thing than we might have supposed? Yes; but that does not mean that it is indestructible. Everybody knows that the more complicated a machine is, the more ways there are in which it can go wrong, and the easier it is to stop it from functioning altogether. And even if we accept all the findings of psychical research at their face value, we should still not be able to deduce from them more than the merest fraction of what the Christian wants to say about life after death. As long ago as the turn of the century, Walter Leaf claimed that:

> the evidence is very striking and very strong. It proves, I think, that memories of the dead survive, and are under special conditions available to us. But I do not see that it proves the survival of what we call the living spirit, the personality.[33]

Many people believe that the cross-correspondences prove more than the fact that the memories of the dead survive; that they show the survival of a living personality, planning intelligently to give proof of its own continuance and to benefit in other ways the whole human race. Even so, what more have they shown than that for a few years after their physical deaths, Myers, Gurney and a few others remained able to communicate with this earth? That they became *immortal* can not be proved. Indeed the evidence is that they communicated for a few years only. What happened then? Was it just that the dissolution of their minds happened a few decades after the dissolution of their bodies? If that is the case, the evidence points to a dismal conclusion. And do we know that everybody survives, or only that it is possible for a few very unusual souls? In other words, the most that the evidence of psychical research, even when interpreted at its most favourable, can *prove*, is that a few people continue capable of retaining contact with the earth for a few years after their death. That they enjoy any kind of *life* (as distinct from mere existence), that it is everlasting, and that it can necessarily be shared by ourselves when our time comes, are gratuitous extensions of the inferences going far beyond the evidence afforded by the facts, or else rest on taking as gospel whatever the mediums (who may be mistaken) tell us is the case.

Our search for proof of human immortality has therefore so far given us a few suggestive pointers which we shall certainly have to take seriously, but still no knock-down certainty.[34] We need to try another line. Christians believe that the resurrection of Jesus of Nazareth is relevant to the matter. We ought therefore to examine it carefully to see whether it makes the case look differently.

4   The resurrection of Jesus

THE case of Jesus the prophet from Nazareth in Galilee is an important one because Christians say that they believe in a life after death because of what happened to him the third day after he was crucified. We must therefore ask whether the biblical writings present us with so strong and irrefutable an historical case for the resurrection of Jesus that we are forced by it to concede that the arguments for human survival of death are made radically different by the results of our historical investigation. If this is at all likely to be the case, clearly we owe it to the biblical records to give them a thorough investigation.

To approach a study of the resurrection through examination of the historical value of the evidence is a method with a long and honourable ancestry. It can hark back to Thomas Woolston's free-thinking *Discourses on the Miracles* of 1729 which concluded, 'I believe, what I have proved, his Resurrection to be a Piece of Fraud, and his other Miracles to have been all Artifice', and which provoked Bishop Thomas Sherlock to produce his *Tryal of the Witnesses of the Resurrection of Jesus*, in which he had no difficulty at all in reaching the diametrically opposite conclusion. It can hark back to Celsus, in the late second century AD, who claimed that belief in the resurrection rested merely on the visions of a semi-hysterical woman, but of whose arguments Origen thought very little.[1] It can, for that matter, hark back to the claim that the disciples stole the body whilst the guard was asleep, which the evangelist (Matt. 28.11–15) takes great trouble in assuring he does not square with the known facts of the case. If we are suspicious that it is only the convinced Christians who can find reasons for affirming the historical veracity of the narratives, and only their opponents who knock the case down, we take refuge in Frank Morison's *Who Moved the Stone?* This famous volume, of almost half a century ago, recently described as 'the most thorough, extended, and in its way convincing example of this approach',[2] was written by a man who set out with the impression that it would be easy to demolish the historical evidence but who found out in the end that the historical evidence had demolished his misgivings.

What Christian apologists have claimed, and what Morison thought he had discovered, was that the evidence of the biblical writers was not as shaky or self-contradictory as was commonly made out, and that those who take the trouble to go through the records with a fine enough tooth-comb will eventually discover all sorts of ways in which the narratives unexpectedly support each other and in which apparently plausible alternatives fall to pieces in their hands as they go rigorously into them. This kind of treatment of the resurrection stories has been called the '*habeas corpus* or detective story approach'.[3] As Sherlock Holmes once remarked, 'when you have eliminated the impossible, whatever remains, *however improbable*, must be the truth'.[4] You eliminate everything more impossible than the fact of a resurrection, and it is the improbable resurrection with which you are left.

Unfortunately for the proponents of this kind of approach[5] the question is not so simply settled. *Habeas corpus* in the matter of the resurrection is having a deal of cold water flung on it at the moment and, curiously enough, most of it comes not from the atheists but from the theologians. No wonder there are some Christians who feel sympathy with the French general who is reported to have said, 'I pray God to protect me from my friends; I can look after my enemies myself.'

To take an example—an extreme one, perhaps, but one from a reputable theologian with a wide readership in academic circles—we may instance the study made by Professor Willi Marxsen. To get as close as he can to the historical bedrock, he goes (quite properly) not to the gospel accounts but to the earlier list given by St Paul in 1 Corinthians. He considers the primary appearance to be, not that to Mary Magdalene which stems from the later accounts, but the one to Simon Peter.[6] In his treatment of it, however, the historical value of this evidence is whittled down and down until the only 'more or less firm historical result' with which we are left is that

> after Good Friday Simon was the first who arrived at faith in Jesus. But we must not phrase this historical conclusion as: Simon was the first to see Jesus. . . . This historical enquiry has not brought us *direct* access to the vision of Simon. The only thing that is historically accessible is Simon's faith, not in the sense of its character as inner event (for this is obviously beyond our reach as well) but in its formative function for the church. . . . I am not denying that Simon saw Jesus. But . . . to the question of what can be established by historical investigation, we can only answer—the faith of Simon as constitutive of the church, and the *assertion* of the early church that this faith was grounded on the seeing of Jesus.[7]

In other words, Marxsen is here claiming that historical investigation cannot bring us proof of the resurrection of Jesus; it cannot even prove that Simon saw Jesus; it cannot even assure us that Simon *believed* he saw Jesus. It can only tell us, as a 'more or less firm historical result', that the early Church asserted that Simon's faith was so founded.

Most English reviewers of Marxsen hold that he has gone too far in loosing the resurrection from its historical moorings and that we can be reasonably sure of a great deal more than he allows; but for the moment let us simply note that there are responsible theologians who can argue that the historical basis for asserting that Jesus was raised from the dead is far from irrefutable. Why should this be so?

The first thing to allow is that there *are* gaps and there *are* discrepancies between the accounts of the resurrection we have in the Bible and that it is inadmissible to gloss over them. For example, who were the women at the tomb? Mary Magdalene alone (John 20.1)? Mary Magdalene and Mary the mother of James (Matt. 28.1)? The two Marys and Salome (Mark 16.1)? Or the two Marys and Joanna (Luke 24.10)? And did they come while it was still dark (John) or about daybreak (Matthew) or very early (Luke) or just after sunrise (Mark)?

And did they see one angel inside the tomb (Mark), one angel sitting on the stone *outside* the tomb (Matthew), or *two* men in dazzling garments inside the sepulchre (Luke)? Did Peter go to the tomb by himself (Luke 24.12) or with the beloved disciple (John 20.3)? Did the ascension take place on the evening of Easter day (Luke in his gospel, 24.50–1) or forty days later (Luke in the Acts of the Apostles, 1.3)? Were the appearances all in Jerusalem (Luke/Acts) or were some in Galilee (Matthew)? And so on. The true, impartial historian knows that it is his duty to recognise these discrepancies and point them out. Only the pseudo-historian with an axe to grind gives certain of his sources the benefit of the doubt (for reasons unconnected with the general historical veracity of the document) and denies it to others, or introduces certain assumptions in order to derive a chronological account from sources which do not seem to be over-interested in chronology.

How could it come about that we should have so many inconsistencies in the records? The first thing to notice is that if we look at the separate accounts in the order in which they were written, we can see the narratives actually growing under our very eyes, and becoming more detailed and more apparently circumstantial the further they get away in time from the event they purport to narrate. Professor R. H. Fuller has made a particularly close study of the matter in his book *The Formation of the Resurrection Narratives* (SPCK, 1972). The interesting point to emerge from his examination is that *narratives* as such were a late development of the Easter gospel. At first the resurrection was not narrated, but simply proclaimed in the one Greek word *egegertai* (he was raised). 'The Easter message is ... earlier than the Easter stories.'[8] But when Paul wrote to the Corinthians, he collected together a number of traditional formulae concerning parts of the gospel he proclaimed ('Christ died for our sins'; 'he was buried'; 'he was raised to life on the third day'), to which he added a series of short lists of resurrection appearances and his own testimony to the risen Christ who appeared to him also (1 Cor. 15.3–8). Professor Fuller believes that these were related in chronological order and that they probably took place over a period of three years or so.

Once we have moved from the single word of announcement of the resurrection gospel to Paul's compilation of lists of appearances, the process has begun; and it continues with a gathering impetus. Mark's account has the same 'feel' as Paul's list. He gives no stories of resurrection-appearances,[9] because he had none to draw on; but he clearly indicates (16.7) that he knew of appearances of the risen Christ only in Galilee and not in Jerusalem. The tradition of the empty tomb and the traditions of the appearances belong to different strata and have not yet been assimilated to one another.

By the time we come to Matthew, there is still very little in the way of *narrative*. It looks to Professor Fuller as though the story of the appearance to the women in Matt. 28.8–10 has developed out of the story in Mark 16.5–8 in which it is an angel rather than the risen Christ who appears in Jerusalem; it is the first stage in the transfer of the stories of appearances of Christ from Galilee to Jerusalem. The narratives of the empty tomb and of the appearances are becoming intertwined.

It is Luke who gives us full-blown narratives, although it is clear from the way in which he inserts 24.34 into the story of the Emmaus disciples ('It is true: the Lord has risen; he has appeared to Simon') that he knew of no details about the appearance to Peter, but only of its inclusion in the traditional list. By the time we get to the touching and feeling of the risen body, and the piece of cooked fish 'which he took and ate before their eyes' (Luke 24.43) the resurrection has ceased to be a pure word of proclamation and has become a quasi-physical matter in which earthly identifying features are being emphasised in the interests of apologetic. And the appearances are by now confined to Jerusalem where the empty tomb is.

The fourth gospel, according to Fuller, has further apologetic and legendary features, such as the mention of the positioning of the grave-clothes (John 20.6–7). The story of the race to the tomb by Peter and the beloved disciple is a correction for Johannine purposes of the account of the primary Petrine appearance.

When we give this kind of treatment to the resurrection accounts, we can see that the case would not have a very high 'evidentiality rating' on Professor Hornell Hart's scale which we discussed in the last chapter (p. 24). The stories as we have them are the result of a long process of accretion, and they date from years after the event to which they bear witness.

This is no new discovery. It has long been common ground amongst New Testament scholars (though the fact seeps through to the pulpits amazingly slowly) that the Gospels were never intended to be chronological accounts of consecutive happenings. Apart from the passion-narratives, they are made up of individual units of earlier tradition, originally circulating independently. The evangelists' accounts cannot be combined into a tightly knit story of the kind which Agatha Christie could dissect to tell us who-dun-it. They take a number of independent traditions, each of which has its own theological point to make, and they only include such of them as make the points about the resurrection which they wish to make, or such as can be moulded to fit their theology. The chronology of the incidents is no concern of theirs.

Thus the sort of question we can sensibly ask of the gospel-writers is not 'what was the original order of events?'—the material for answering that question has been lost for ever—but 'what is the individual gospel-writer (or what were his sources) intending to get across to the reader by the anecdotes he relates and the way in which he tells them?' In the the words of Professor C. F. Evans:

> It is not simply difficult to harmonise these traditions, but quite impossible. . . . For what have to be combined are not a number of scattered pieces from an originally single matrix, but separate expressions of the Easter faith. Each of these is complete in itself; each has developed along its own line so as to serve in the end as a proper conclusion for an evangelist of his own particular version of the gospel. . . . Each evangelist gives his own version as a total version, which was not intended to stand up only if it stood alongside another, or was supplemented by another.[10]

Habeas corpus, then, has had its day. Yet that does not mean that we can salvage nothing of historical value from the gospel records of the resurrection. Professor Fuller has done well to remind us that there is an undoubted development of the narrative element from Paul's list to Luke's and John's stories, and that the later the account the more detail there is in it. But we know from the most cursory reading of Paul's letters that he has precious little to tell us in the way of biographical details about the life and death of Jesus, so it is not surprising that he shows no interest in the narrative element of the resurrection. There is no *a priori* reason why the later evangelists could not be drawing upon very primitive traditions of the resurrection narratives, accurately remembered and handed down in their pre-literary days. The details of the resurrection story may be questionable, but the central event to which they bear witness is a different matter. And there are to be found New Testament scholars of critical skill and radical scholarship who still maintain that our evidence for there having been a resurrection is as good as that for any incident in the history of the ancient world.

Professor Evans, for example, begins his argument from the fact that, in the writings of the time shortly before Jesus, we meet with a bewildering variety of beliefs about the future life which are by no means mutually consistent or even coherent.[11] Most people take this to indicate that a belief in the future life was widespread and well-established in Judaism by the time of our Lord. But a very different conclusion could be drawn, and clearly it is one to which Professor Evans himself inclines. The intertestamental literature with its interest in speculation about resurrection is only:

> that which has happened to survive, and its very survival may be due to the interest in it of later Jews and Christians, who, from their own point of view, were concerned with what it had to say. It is not altogether clear how far the views it expresses were widely held. . . . Its very incoherence could argue that resurrection was not a universally held belief and badge of orthodoxy, but a subject of considerable speculation and debate.[12]

Among the evidence for this view, Professor Evans cites the fact that the Sadducees did not believe in a resurrection (see Acts 23.8; Mark 12.18)—their literature perished after the sack of Jerusalem in AD 70—the fact that the Dead Sea Scrolls do not, in his view, show any belief in resurrection, and the fact that Mark 9.10 can show that the disciples could ask among themselves 'what this "rising from the dead" could mean'. It is certain that though the first three Gospels are written by people who believe in the resurrection and who might therefore have been expected to include in their account anything which would reinforce this faith and show that it was at least consonant with the teaching of Jesus himself, they show Jesus as having very little indeed to say on this subject. All this points Professor Evans to the conclusion that:

> if the doctrine of resurrection was not firmly fixed in Judaism, and if it is largely absent from the teaching of Jesus, then particular attention is focused on the actual resurrection of Jesus. It may be suggested that only this event, whatever it may have been, could have brought it about that there emerged in Christianity a precise, confident and articulate faith in which resurrection has moved from the circumference to the centre.

It is therefore possible for a critical historian to claim that he can rescue more material of historical value from the New Testament accounts than Marxsen or Fuller allow.[13] But we still have to ask ourselves whether this incident from first-century Palestine can bear the weight we are trying to put on it. Do we honestly think that the account of the alleged appearance on a number of occasions and to a number of people of the recently crucified Rabbi or prophet called Jesus of Nazareth is a convincing argument for asserting that any other man may expect to continue his existence after his physical death? The evidence is of such a quality that the experts themselves disagree as to how much of it is worth historical credence, and even if we were to accept all of it with uncritical credulity, we have already seen from the chapter on psychical research that the postulate of human immortality by no means necessarily follows from it. So we must again confess at the end of a chapter that the certainty which we have been demanding has eluded us.

5   The neglected factor

WE have been looking for certainty as to the fate of human
beings after death, and so far our search seems to be proving a
peculiarly unsatisfactory one. The arguments and evidence at
which we have looked have given us at the most an ambiguous
and uncertain case. The philosophical arguments have been
finely poised; the data of psychical research must not be
ignored, but they have been subject to more than one
explanation and cannot in any case take us as far as we want
to go; even the resurrection of Jesus the prophet from Nazareth
in Galilee could be seen as little more than an interesting but
ultimately insignificant piece of very ancient history—one
more item in an article on 'Supernormal phenomena in
classical antiquity'.[1] Have we therefore reached stalemate?

Yes; but what we have so far examined has not been a waste
of time. We shall be seeing its importance and significance
soon; but not until we have found the proper direction from
which to approach it. Each one of us must have known of
intractable problems on which light has consistently refused to
come; then we step aside and realise that the problem can be
tackled from an entirely different standpoint, and at last there
is a possibility of real progress. Something of this kind must
have happened to astronomy in the time of Copernicus. It was
becoming more and more difficult to account for the movement
of the sun and planets round the earth. The system of spheres
and of spheres within spheres had become quite impossibly
complicated. Then Copernicus stood aside from this way of
looking at things, and adopted a new standpoint, with the sun
at the centre and the earth and the planets revolving round it.
All the difficulties did not disappear at a stroke, but so many of
them did that Copernicus saw that the only hope for any

progress in astronomy lay in abandoning the earth-centred viewpoint and in adopting the one which took the sun as the centre. That Copernicus was right has been vindicated by the whole story of astronomy from his time onwards.

Or again, how many of us have worried at some problem or other and seen no way out of it, and then suddenly realised that we had left a vital factor out of consideration—a factor which was the clue to the whole mystery? Biology in the eighteenth century was like astronomy before Copernicus. There was a mass of data but no pattern to the mass. The bewildering variety of living creatures could be classified, but the classifications did not make a great deal of sense. But once the dogma of the fixity of species was abandoned, and the crucial importance of the new factor of random variation was realised, the way lay open for Darwin and Wallace to produce the revolutionary concept of evolution by natural selection. That new factor, hitherto unrecognised, was the key to the whole mystery.

Something of the same kind has been happening to us so far. We need a new standpoint; we have missed the vital factor, and therefore we are stuck.

It is the contention of Christians that the neglected factor is God, and that the new perspective we need is an inescapably theological one. The Christian is not surprised that, in the matter of human destiny, arguments which leave God out of consideration are inconclusive. Christian convictions are reached primarily on a Christian understanding of the nature and activities of God, and Christians do not expect non-theistic arguments about human destiny to be very successful in generating much conviction. That even goes for arguments about the alleged resurrection of Jesus of Nazareth. For the Christian, the resurrection appearances are only significant if Jesus is someone a great deal more than 'the prophet from Nazareth in Galilee'. That resurrection of his only makes sense as part of a coherent scheme if it is in character with the God whom Jesus came to reveal to us; if, in fact, it is seen as a mighty act of the living God and as pivotal in the whole scheme of man's salvation.

To establish whether this is so will involve asking questions about who Jesus was and why the things that happened to him are qualitatively more significant than things which might have happened to any other man—even to any other prophet. The Christian is not overmuch concerned with the Easter story if it cannot be put into a much wider and more theologically meaningful context than would satisfy the person who is investigating it simply as an historical record of an alleged paranormal occurrence from the distant past. It is only when we admit its centrality within a faith which claims certain things about the character of God and about the relations of Jesus to the Godhead that the case begins to look different; as different as astronomy did to Plato and to Copernicus.

This does not mean that our excursions into philosophy and psychical research and history have been irrelevant. What it *does* do is to alter the nature of their relevance.

The Christian can read the evidence summarised in the opening chapters of this book, and remain unworried by the doubts and qualifications they (properly) express. More than this, he can find a positive satisfaction in the very uncertainty of purely humanistic and non-theistic attempts to prove human survival. The Christian would wish to argue from an entirely opposite direction. He would begin with God; with his experience; with what sort of a God he was; with the nature of his relations towards mankind; with his attitude towards the human individual; with his actions in and with and through Jesus of Nazareth. Having reached his conviction along some such lines as this, the Christian could then go to these philosophical and parapsychological arguments—which he realises are inconclusive on their own—and take them as corroborative evidence. In other words, although he could not go to them for an independent and knock-down proof of human immortality, he can nonetheless approach the arguments of the philosophers and the data of the parapsychologists with a mind which is readier to give them the benefit of the doubt than would be the strictly logical humanist's. He now sees them as corroborative of faith rather than determinative of an argument.

Perhaps we ought to take an example or two in order to make the point clear. Earlier on (p. 16) we read how Bertrand

Russell had written that 'belief in survival arose as an emotional reaction to the fact of death' and that 'we have no right to expect the Universe to adapt itself to our emotions'. That all depends upon what we believe about the Universe. If we believe that it is mindless or purposeless—even if we believe it was made by a scornful and sadistic tantalising mocker—we would be inclined to accept the force of Russell's argument. But if we believe that that hunger for immortality, that feeling that our life would be meaningless if death cancelled everything we strove for and everything we achieved and everything we had so laboriously and costingly learned in the course of our three score years and ten—if we believe that that emotion was put into man's heart by the God who made the Universe (and who made the men within it), then our beliefs about that God would be highly relevant to our beliefs about human survival.

Those who believe that the Universe was made by a just and loving God who also made man and all his desires, and that God did not plant those desires within man simply to tantalise and mock him, have a right to expect the Universe to adapt itself to these emotions of ours—or at any rate to be the sort of Universe where these emotions are at home. A just Creator will not give us a hunger which is all for nothing. To a believer in the Christian God, man's deepest desires are a clue to the very nature of reality. 'Thou hast made us unto thyself', said St Augustine to his God, 'and our hearts are restless until they find their rest in thee.'[2] God could not be the sort of God whom the Christians affirm him to be if he had created men with such immortal longings and then mocked at the aspirations he had himself planted in their hearts by snuffing a man out like a spent candle at the end of his earthly life.

But yet this faith of the Christian is not without support from external facts, such as the data of psychical research. The Christian is in a maddeningly 'heads-I-win, tails-you-lose' position with respect to them. Their positive interpretation confirms the Christian attitude, but their negative interpretation does not destroy it. We need to spell this position out and to give an example or two.

The Christian believes in a life after death. But there is

nothing in his faith which insists that there is any communication between this world and the next except communion in spiritual companionship and prayer. Anything more than (or other than) that is a matter for empirical testing; not for the pronouncements of dogma. So if every glimmer of light that psychical research promises to shed on this subject proves in the final analysis to be a will-o'-the-wisp, the Christian's withers will remain unwrung. He will not conclude that the dead do not survive, but only that they do not communicate with us in the way that some psychical researchers thought they did. On the other hand, if the Christian wants to read the casebook of psychical research without an attitude of sceptical negativity, he will find it possible to be drawn towards conclusions which are not in conflict with his Christian faith. He will discover a great deal to support his basic Christian conviction that the end of this life is not the end of human existence and in addition he may come to hold opinions about details of the future life on which the Christian religion as such has no pronouncement to make—one way or the other.

This will not absolve him from the duty to ask critical questions about the phenomena, and it will not mean that he will accept everything at its face value—he will still have to ask of every case presented to him, 'Is this good evidence for post-mortem activity or is it more likely in this case that the normal explanation is to be preferred to the paranormal?'; and he will certainly need to 'test the spirits, to see whether they are from God' (1 John 4.1). It *will* absolve him from the effort to find and to prefer a non-paranormal explanation (however far-fetched) to the explanation which is *prima facie* the most likely.

It might be useful now to see how this might work out in practice. At the end of Chapter 3, we recognised that it would be entirely in accord with the data to hold the opinion that some favoured personalities may be able to communicate with the living for some little while after their death; but that eventually, even for them, some time after the dissolution of their bodies, the dissolution of their psyches takes place. Some people can survive for longer than others, but eventually we all fall back into nothingness. That is one way to take the data.

But, with the same set of data in front of us, we can make a very different set of inferences.

We can, for example, argue that although every person survives death, not every departed soul wishes to communicate and not all who are willing are able. The fact that messages come only from the few need not mean that only the few survive. Perhaps only a minority who have died wish to keep up their links with loved ones still on this earth, and only a minority out of that minority either have the special psychical constitution which enables them to do this, or have loved ones who want to make the particular arrangements which are necessary with a psychic sensitive. Imagine the frustration of a departed spirit who has something he wishes to communicate, and yet for whom the necessary channels from this side are not made available. This may have been what happened in the case of Jim Pike.[3]

Jim was the son of Bishop Pike, at that time Bishop of California. Not many days after Jim's tragic death in February 1966, there began a series of strange poltergeist disturbances around the bishop and his friends. Eventually, these became so upsetting that the bishop talked them over with acquaintances who knew something about parapsychology. They suggested that he should sit with a sensitive. Immediately, messages came through, purporting to be from Jim. Further study and further sittings eventually convinced the initially sceptical bishop that the messages were genuine. We may imagine Jim using the method of causing poltergeist disturbances in order to get his father to contact the sort of person who would be able to put him in touch. Otherwise Bishop Pike, who previously had neither knowledge nor experience of mediumship (nor sympathy with it) would certainly never have consulted a sensitive, and Jim would never have been able to pass on to his father the messages that he was wanting to give.

We could therefore accept the hypothesis that, although all survive, only a few communicate. We could go further. One reading of the evidence is that, since messages from a particular person gradually stop coming through, this indicates that his psyche is gradually disintegrating until it reaches the point where there is nothing left with which to communicate.

This, however, is not the only possible reading of the evidence. We could just as well suppose that the life of the world to come is a progressive life. Those of the departed who communicate with us have at length to cut the umbilical cord which still attaches them emotionally to this earth. When this has been done, they are able to move on, progressing to a further stage, in which their sights are directed towards other goals than keeping in touch with their earthly loved ones. This certainly is the impression gained by Bishop Pike in the communications purporting to be from his son and received over the course of a couple of years through three different mediums.

> In the first two sessions ... the impression I received was that Jim ... deeply regretted that he took his own life. He was confused and suffering, and concerned about whether we would judge him for what he had done ... During the next year he seemed to move on to a new level where he felt more or less neutral about what the future might hold for him. He was particularly anxious to convince me (and, through me, the rest of the family) that he lives on, and he began to be able to show concern for others. ... When almost two years had passed from the time of his death, he apparently had found a specific role on the other side ('I have been given the job of helping those who come over after having committed suicide—it's because I understand'), and the need to be in communication with me seemed reduced. ... And finally, for the first time he was able to say he was genuinely happy.[4]

Indeed, this is a very natural thing to suppose. We are who we are not only because of our heavenward-directed urges, but also (and very largely) because of the loves we have, the attachments we make, the companionships and interests we share, on this earth. Detach a man completely from all existing human contacts, and from his desire for such contacts, and he becomes not more of a man, but less. The fact of death is traumatic, but however traumatic it is we need not expect it to destroy in a person all interest in those he has left behind and all desire to remain in touch with them. Admittedly, as he becomes more at home in his new world, so his interests will change and his goals be modified; but we would expect this to happen over a period of time rather than in the twinkling of an eye. It is a little like emigration. The new arrival in Australia feels homesick. He writes to friends back in England and thinks about them a great deal. Then, gradually, he finds his feet in his new country, makes new friends there, gets drawn into plans for his new future, and begins slowly to think more often about Australia and what lies ahead, and less often about England and his past. He would be heartless if, on arrival, he was not drawn towards his friends who remained behind in the old country. He would be foolish if he did not eventually transfer his affections to his new surroundings.

This example should have shown us how the same set of data can be fitted into two very different frameworks. The sceptic believes at most in a delayed dissolution of the personality after death for those few whose personality is not dissolved immediately. Others see the data as supporting the view that some of the departed are willing and able to communicate, but that even they gradually shift their interest away from earth and towards their new environment. The former hypothesis is not likely to be acceptable to a Christian; but then it is not the only inference which may be drawn from the data. The second hypothesis is consistent with the data and may be held without contradicting the Christian faith. So the Christian knows which way to interpret the ambiguous data.

Some people will be deeply suspicious of the turn which the argument has taken in this chapter. Is religion being used to bolster up a bad argument, to clinch a case which is not good enough to win its way by its own inherent quality? No. There is still good evidence and bad evidence, and the Christian will want to be as firm as anyone else in rejecting the latter. Christianity is not credulity, and sanctimonious hogwash will not convert fraudulent or misinterpreted evidence into acceptable data. What we are saying is that even the best data can be interpreted in more than one way; but that when the possibilities are as evenly balanced as we have seen them to be on this matter, the Christian will have additional reasons for thinking that the scale ought to tip in one direction rather than the other. If we refuse to let God into the argument, the only thing of which we can be certain is our own uncertainty; but if we approach the question of human destiny in the light of a Christian knowledge of God, the balance of probability shifts decisively towards one of the two options between which we were previously unable rationally to choose.

All the same, there may be a feeling that these were not the kind of arguments for survival which people expected. 'You ask me', a person says, 'to assume the existence of the Christian God as though that were everything, and then human survival appears as a mere by-product of that belief. What we wanted was an argument for immortality which begins with mortal man and ends with his immortal soul, and then goes on to draw irrefutable conclusions about the nature and character of discarnate life.' That only shows how constantly and consistently people get things right-about-face. Man's immortality is not something arrived at from a study of man, as though man were the be-all and end-all of the Universe, and God some external source of power brought in merely to ensure man's safe continuance within that Universe. Man's immortality is something which stems from the answer to the questions, 'Who is God? What has he made man for? Is he powerful enough to see his purposes stand?'

This means, also, that it is not possible to argue for immortality on one's own terms. It is necessary to see what Christianity has to say about it, and accept that God comes first, and that our continued existence is bound up with his plans for the totality of all things—in other words, with Christian theology as a whole.

Once take *that* viewpoint, and we find ourselves talking about something incredibly richer than we could ever have expected from our incursions into philosophy, psychical research, and history. What strikes the Christian about some of the sayings of non-Christians on this subject is not that they are wrong, but that they are unutterably *dull*. For instance, here is what a distinguished scientist half a century ago had to say in the course of his arguments against the idea of human survival of death:

Truth, under the profound veils which cover it, must be far

more noble than this antiquated idea—*the prolongation of our miserable individual intellectuality....* The theory of survival ... must be held to constitute only a revival of very ancient superstitions.[5]

The Christian's first reaction to that might well be to jump up in annoyed self-defence. An antiquated idea, indeed! The revival of very ancient superstitions! But second thoughts may lead us to ask what precisely these antiquated ideas and ancient superstitions are. 'The prolongation of our miserable individual intellectuality'; an idea so dull, so self-centred, so coldly cerebral that it is no wonder that the very humanity of a man recoils from it. That is the trouble with the evidence of psychical research considered on its own. The *most* it can decisively *prove* is so little: one or two individuals holding on to their disintegrating self-consciousness for a short time after their physical deaths. The belief that all men can be immortal, and that heaven consists in the un-self-regarding and social delights of the company of him whom our souls were created to love, is as different from that as chalk from cheese. That these limited, frustrated, and unsatisfactory lives of ours are going to continue unchanged for generations to come would not necessarily be good news; it could well be the worst news ever.[6] If the resurrection life were simply this present life continued, Paradise were wilderness enow. But this is not the Christian's belief, because he holds that God who made us for immortality did not make us for a destiny that was dull and boring. He made us to be alive. A Christian's faith adds a whole new dimension of zest and aliveness to the humanistic conception of immortality—the relish without which heaven would be (quite literally) purgatory.

'But', you complain, 'we have asked for certainty and all we have been offered is faith!' Precisely. We have been offered faith. Faith in God. The matter is rather like Euclidean geometry or formal logic. If you ask for a proof of some theorem, I must give it you in terms of some premises from which the proof begins. The theorem cannot be proved from no premises at all, and still less can it be proved from any or every arbitrary set of premises. It is my contention (and the whole of this book so far has been devoted to trying to make this contention good) that the only premises from which the argument about human destiny can go—and get anywhere—are Christian ones about the nature of God. Once those are accepted, and the argument followed up, then we shall know how to interpret the ambiguous evidences which have been discussed in Chapters 2 to 4 of this book. We shall see them as corroborative of the Christian claim, and as indications that Christianity cannot be wide of the mark. The Christian claim is reasonable.

That does not mean that it can be argued from neutral evidences, as natural theology is in danger of trying to say. What it does mean is that Christian theology does not conflict with the empirical evidence of the world around us, and that this evidence can, without contortion, be interpreted along lines consistent with the Christian revelation. That is why it is important that the 'natural' evidence for a continued human life after death should be surveyed, and why we shall be returning from time to time in this book to the data of psychical studies; but that is also why we should not expect this evidence on its own to produce certainty. If it did, then Christian truth could be cut off from Christian premises, and Christian faith and the Christian life would be unnecessary.

This book is inviting you to stake your life on, and put your faith in, the Christian God; it aims to show you what this involves in terms of your eternal destiny. Any other way of persuading men of their immortality would be false, and making claims which could not be substantiated. I cannot expect anyone to be compelled towards a belief in human survival without first accepting a Christian view of God and his relation to the world and to the men in it; but once accept such a view, and the audacious simplicity of Paul's words stands self-apparent: 'God not only raised our Lord from the dead; he will also raise us by his power. . . . If the dead are not raised, it follows that Christ was not raised. . . . But the truth is, Christ was raised to life—the firstfruits of the harvest of the dead'(1 Cor. 6.14; 15.16,20). To put it in a nutshell, I believe in the resurrection of the dead and the life of the world to come; but I only believe in that resurrection and that life because I believe in one God the Father almighty, maker of heaven and earth, and in one Lord Jesus Christ, his only Son, our resurrection and our life.

6   God and resurrection

THE Old Testament tells us very little about what the individual may expect after death. In most of it, we see Jehovah as very much a god of this life, whose concerns are with the men who live on this earth and the things which happen to them on it. Indeed, any other sort of God would never have earned his people's allegiance, nor in the internecine tribal wars of the time would he long have *had* a people to give him allegiance. When Sennacherib, King of Assyria, attacked the fortified cities of Judah, he sent his chief officer to King Hezekiah at Jerusalem to persuade him that it was no good trying to resist the Assyrian armies. The strongest argument in his case was that the Assyrian god had been *proved* to be more powerful than any of the gods of any of the other nations. 'Hezekiah', he claimed to the people of Jerusalem,

> will only mislead you by telling you that the LORD will save you. Did the god of any of these nations save his land from the king of Assyria? Where are the gods of Hamath and Arpad? Where are the gods of Sepharvaim, Hena, and Ivvah? Where are the gods of Samaria? Did they save Samaria from me? Among all the gods of the nations is there one who saved his land from me? And how is the LORD to save Jerusalem? (2 Kgs 18.32–5)

The proud boast was intended to strike terror into the followers of the God of Judah, and it was only because Jehovah proved his power by striking the Assyrian armies (a plague claimed 185,000 men in a single night, if we are to believe the chronicles) that his sovereignty was acknowledged.

There was at that time some conception of a future life, but

when we look at it, it only confirms the belief that the writ of
Jehovah ran in this world only. When a man died, his shade or
shadow went to the realm of She'ol where existence was little
more than vegetative and where the joy of Jehovah's presence
was certainly unknown. The Psalmist in his misery complains
to God that he has 'become like a man beyond help, like a man
who lies dead or the slain who sleep in the grave, whom thou
rememberest no more because they are cut off from thy care'
(Ps. 88.4,5). The grave, for him, is the place of destruction, the
dark, the land of oblivion (Ps. 88.11,12). The Greeks had the
same kind of doctrine which they expressed by the idea of
Hades, a grey place of hopelessness where you could hardly
speak of the shades as being either dead or alive. No wonder
the preacher said that 'a live dog is better than a dead lion'
because 'the dead know nothing. There are no more rewards
for them; they are utterly forgotten' (Eccles. 9.4,5). Indeed, it
was better to be a living slave than a dead king, for in that
dismal existence, not even a king has any position of power.
Isaiah sings a taunting song against the great King of Babylon,
and imagines the scene when he dies and meets the shades in
the nether world:

> Sheol below was all astir
> > to meet you at your coming;
> > she roused the ancient dead to meet you,
> > all who had been leaders on earth;
> > she made all who had been kings of the nations
> > rise from their thrones.
> One and all they greet you with these words:
> > So you too are weak as we are,
> > and have become one of us! (Isa. 14.9–10)

This simple theology—that God was both willing and able
to reward in this life those nations who served him and to
punish those who defied him—would not stand up to the facts.
The realisation dawned slowly, mainly because the ancient
Israelites (like the ancient world in general) thought more in
terms of the nation and of corporate identity than of individual
identity. We who live in the individualistic West of the
twentieth century find it hard to make the mental journey to a

place and an age where this is true, but we shall not properly understand the thought-world of the Old Testament unless we make the effort. Individual righteous men might meet an untimely death, but they lived on in their sons, and God would not forsake his people as a whole. Thus it was a greater and more terrible fate to threaten a man with the extinction of all his descendants than to put him to death as an individual; and there are gruesome stories in the Old Testament and elsewhere of the slaughter of whole tribes and families, whose gods perished with them because, once the tribe had disappeared, the god had no one left to serve him.

The growth of a belief in individual reward and retribution caused the difficulties in this doctrine to be highlighted. We can see it starting in the time of Ezekiel:

> It is the soul that sins, and no other, that shall die; a son shall not share a father's guilt, nor a father his son's. The righteous man shall reap the fruit of his own righteousness, and the wicked man the fruit of his own wickedness (Ezek. 18.20).

Fine words; but they would not wash. They led to a rewriting of history by the Deuteronomistic school (in the best traditions of Orwell's *1984*) which produced an entirely moralistic, frequently biased, and sometimes fictitious history of the kingdoms of Israel and Judah, and to such impossible statements as 'I have been young and am now grown old, and never have I seen a righteous man forsaken' (Ps. 37.25); or 'You who fear the Lord, expect prosperity, lasting happiness and favour. Consider the past generations and see: was anyone who trusted the Lord ever disappointed?' (Ecclus 2.9,10). To which the answer was: I have considered, and the reply is *yes*! Hence the agonisings of the Book of Job.

The crunch came in the Maccabean risings of the second century BC, of which one of the literary monuments is the Book of Daniel. It could not be—it just could not be—that those who had so bravely given their life for the cause of the God of Israel should perish as though they had never been. There had to be a recompense for the individual as well as a promise of permanence and restoration for the nation. The belief in She'ol still continued, but it began to be considered that perhaps She'ol might not last for ever; at least, not in everybody's case. At some moment in the future, at the close of human history, God would act in a mighty drama.

At that moment your people will be delivered, every one who is written in the book: many of those who sleep in the dust of the earth will wake, some to everlasting life and some to the reproach of eternal abhorrence (Dan 12.1–2).

That, of course, was in the future, and it does not seem to refer to all the shades of all the dead, but only to the best and the worst of the Israelites:

those who had performed superlatively well by resisting the tyrant to the death, who are to be resurrected to life, and those who had apostatized from Judaism, who are to be resurrected to 'abhorrence'.[1]

Meanwhile, awaiting this decisive act of God, the shades of the dead were still in She'ol, just as Samuel was when he was called up by the medium from En-dor (1 Sam. 28.3–20). That is why the early Christians believed that Jesus needed to go and preach the release of the resurrection to 'the imprisoned spirits' (1 Pet. 3.19) who were waiting for this great and final deliverance.

What was envisaged in this advance of thought during the Maccabean ferment was nothing like 'heaven' as later Christian thought has elaborated it. It was, quite simply, a restoration to this life so that the martyrs could be reunited with their brethren and take their place in the kingdom on earth. Admittedly, when this happened, there would begin a life in which God was universally acknowledged and glorified and in which his enemies would be put firmly and permanently out of the way, so that it would be a golden age: but the restoration of the slain to earth was conceived in a very literal and material manner. This comes out particularly clearly in the gruesome story of the martyr Razis. At the moment of arrest he tried to commit suicide by falling on his sword, but missed his aim. So he fished around in the wound, 'took his entrails in both hands and flung them at the crowd. And thus, invoking the Lord of life and breath to give these entrails back to him again, he died' (2 Macc. 14.46).

During the two centuries between the Maccabean literature and the times of the New Testament, there was a bewildering variety of speculation within Judaism about the after-life. Was there to be a resurrection of righteous Israelites only, or resurrection of both righteous and unrighteous, followed by a sifting out in judgement? If the latter, was it to be a resurrection of all men or of Israelites only? You pick your writer and you take your choice. As C. F. Evans points out:

> there are differences about place (resurrection to earth, to a renewed earth, to Paradise), time (to a messianic period belonging to this age, to eternal life in perpetuity), and form (a reconstituted body, a transformed body, without body). These variations, some of them sometimes found within a single work, reflect a considerable fluidity of thought, which was probably brought about by the impact upon Israel of new modes of belief.[2]

We may add to his catalogue a more 'philosophical' doctrine, closely akin to the teaching of Socrates already quoted (pp. 12–13), and which may be found in the book of the Wisdom of Solomon. According to that, man (or perhaps only the righteous man?) is inherently immortal and cannot die.

> The souls of the just are in God's hand, and torment shall not touch them. In the eyes of foolish men they seemed to be dead; their departure was reckoned as defeat, and their going from us as disaster. But they are at peace, for though in the sight of men they may be punished, they have a sure hope of immortality; and after a little chastisement they will receive great blessings (Wisd. 3.1–5).

There is more than one interpretation of the significance of this ferment of new ideas. They may indicate that at that time virtually everybody agreed in some form of future life for some people beyond She'ol, though there was great debate about the details. It is more likely that the documents which happen to have survived are simply the literary remains of advanced thinkers, unrepresentative of the people as a whole. We have already quoted Professor Evans's opinion that at this period, 'resurrection was not a universally held belief and badge of orthodoxy, but a subject of considerable speculation and debate'. Resurrection was not a subject with which the Jewish religion was over-concerned. It was a doctrine which 'did not belong to the main stream of "biblical" religion'.[3]

And then came Jesus of Nazareth.

Let us start with two sayings of his. 'Are not sparrows five for twopence? And yet not one of them is overlooked by God. More than that, even the hairs of your head have all been counted. Have no fear; you are worth more than any number of sparrows' (Luke 12.6–7). That is the first fact: God cares. And the second is that he is able. When Jesus was disputing over the resurrection with the unbelieving Sadducees, he said to them, 'You are mistaken, and surely this is the reason: you do not know either the scriptures or the power of God' (Mark 12.24). The basis of Jesus' assurance of the destiny of man lies not in his doctrine of man, but in his doctrine of God. God cares, and God can. The God who created mankind loves us even more than we care for ourselves; and it is not man in the mass for which he is concerned, but each unique individual. He cares for each man's thirst for what is good and true and beautiful, and with each individual's attempt to live in closer companionship with him. It is not that as we advance in the Christian life we are more and more assured of the inherent value of the human soul, so that we cannot conceive of God's destroying anything so pure and so beautiful. In fact, the opposite happens: a Christian as he strives towards God becomes more and more convinced of the evil in himself and the corruptibility of human nature, so that he is tempted to look at his own soul and despair. Despite that, the Christian finds himself being led into a relationship with God which seems to him, in the words of the Collect,[4] to be more than either he desires or deserves. He knows himself cared for by God, and he finds in that relationship something ultimate and therefore permanent. It is what he discovers about God rather than what he discovers about himself which gives him his ground of hope.

The Spirit has created a relationship between us and God which makes itself felt as having no temporal terminus at all. We know that we shall always be loved of God. We know this, not because of anything about us, but because it is God who loves us. We know he will hold us forever in his hand. We know this, not because it is we who are held, but because it is his hand which holds us. We know that we cannot drift beyond his care, not because we see an end to how far we can wander or be carried, but because we know his care can be subject to no limits whatever. Nothing can separate us from the love of God, neither life nor death.[5]

This is an emphasis which comes out in the whole of the teaching of Jesus. In his recorded words, there is remarkably little in terms of sheer volume about life after death; but there is a great deal about God, the Kingdom of God (or of heaven), and the crisis of choice in which this kingdom puts men. 'Many of the parables which seem to speak of future judgement are seen on closer consideration to be parables of crisis.'[6] The crisis is a crisis of spiritual and eternal dimensions. Jesus believed that in his ministry the forces of God and the forces of evil were poised for their final confrontation, and that it was a matter of eternal importance to a man on which side he stood. That this involved a time beyond this present earthly era is clear, but about the details of it very much less is said. A great deal of what there is, comes in the form of incidental *obiter dicta* rather than as the main thrust of the parable which contains it; but that Jesus believed in eternal life is made clear in such sayings as Matt. 25.46—'the righteous will enter eternal life'—and in his reply to the Sadducees, where they are trying to make him look foolish with a trick question about a woman who had seven husbands. When they rise from the dead, says Jesus, men and women are like angels in heaven. God, who is the God of Abraham and Isaac and Jacob, is not the God of the dead but of the living (Mark 12.25–7). It is also instructive to look at sayings of Jesus where the future life is simply assumed and a mention of it is slipped in *en passant* in the course of a word about some other topic altogether; an example occurs in Luke 14.14 with the phrase 'on the day when good men rise from the dead'.

So much for the *words* of Jesus. The case for taking him seriously rests upon his *actions* too. Death is not something that a Christian can treat lightly. It cannot be trivialised. It is the domain of Satan. It is the irrational, that which breaks up in a moment what has been built up in a lifetime, which mocks at human effort and progress and rationality. The gospels tell us that Jesus came to challenge Satan—to build up where Satan destroyed, to bring life and order where Satan wished there to be death and chaos. There was a struggle going on during the ministry of Jesus, and it was going on at a deeper than human level. That was the significance of the mighty works which accompanied the ministry: the strong man was being tied up (Mark 3.27), and someone stronger than him was coming upon him to overpower him (Luke 11.22). Jesus was the expected One who was to come, and this was shown by the fact that around him the blind were recovering their sight, the lame were walking, lepers were being made clean, the deaf were hearing, and the poor were being told the good news of the coming Kingdom (Matt. 11.5); the stammerers spoke plainly (Mark 7.31–7, fulfilling Isa. 35.6) and the demons acknowledged their master (Mark 5.1–12). Finally, to show that he could challenge Satan at the very throne of his kingdom of darkness and despair, Jesus raised Jairus' daughter and the son of the widow from Nain and Lazarus from Bethany (Mark 5.21–43; Luke 7.11–17; John 11.1–44), so that he could truly claim to have watched Satan fall like lightning out of the sky (Luke 10.18) and to be himself the resurrection and life (John 11.25).

If we, reading the gospels through twentieth-century spectacles, cannot believe that these things actually happened, or that they were not exaggerated and misreported accounts, we must still acknowledge that they are accounts of what the early Christians believed Jesus to have done and that it is (in part at least) because of the things which happened in the ministry of Jesus that his early followers came to believe that he was no ordinary man. In this estimate of him, the Christian claims that they were right. If they were *not*, it is hard to build up a convincing case for our own future destiny. This is because that case does not depend solely on the sayings of Jesus and his power. It also depends—quite crucially—upon who Jesus was and is, upon what God was doing in and through him, and upon our continuing relationship with this person in whom the demonic forces were meeting their match. In other words, the destiny of man not only demands God for its certain solution; it also demands God in Christ. We cannot reach certainty on the subject if we start from man's end; but if we start from God's end we are bound to have to wrestle with the figure of Jesus and his relation to the Godhead. Theology is not sufficient without Christology. If it is true that we are not risen without God, it is even more true that we are not risen without Christ. What this means will be argued more fully in later chapters; for the present let us simply record that the Christian solution to the question of human destiny involves coming to terms with the fact of who Jesus is. And whatever you believe about his earthly life or on whatever aspects of the story of the ministry you disbelieve or suspend judgement, there is one thing about him which is so central to the whole case that suspension of judgement is fatal. That is the question of what happened to him in the end.

Could such a person—in whom the power of God was seen so signally to be working—himself be bound by the strongest power of Satan? On the Sabbath after his crucifixion, the disciples feared as much. 'We *had* been hoping', they wistfully said to one another, 'that he was the man to liberate Israel' (Luke 24.21). It was the conviction of the earliest disciples, and it has been the conviction of countless disciples since, that by a mighty act of the living God, Jesus—who had passed to She'ol—yet returned to this earth where he showed himself to his disciples and gave ample proof that he was alive (Acts 1.3) before taking his place in the presence of God himself, there to die no more. What was so staggering about this claim was that it concerned a single individual and it was before the end of the world. If the disciples had expected Jesus to rise, it would have been 'at the resurrection on the last day' (John 11.24).

There existed an expectation that the end of the world would bring a resurrection of *all* the dead along with a general judgment. Neither the disciples nor anyone else expected the resurrection of *one* person alone. Without a new, compelling reason they would not have asserted the individual resurrection of Jesus.[7]

Resurrection is a thing of the last day, not a thing to be expected (even of the Christ) in the here and now. That is what led Paul to assert that we who live between the resurrection of Christ and the Last Day are living in 'the overlap of the ages'.[8]

What, then, is this thing called 'resurrection' which we postulate of Jesus? And what is its relation to the historical facts which we investigated in Chapter 4 above? We saw there that if we were minded to say that the historical evidence for the resurrection of Jesus of Nazareth was not good enough to be regarded as proof, we should not be violating the canons of historical research. But could we have *any* historical evidence for a resurrection? Is resurrection anything that could be proved by historical reconstruction, however watertight?

There is an account in the document known as the *Gospel of Peter* which purports to give a description of what happened on the first Easter Day. It is a trifle long-winded, but the central section of it runs as follows:

Now in the night in which the Lord's day dawned, when the soldiers, two by two in every watch, were keeping guard, there rang out a loud voice in heaven, and they saw the heavens opened and two men come down from there in a great brightness and draw nigh to the sepulchre. That stone which had been laid against the entrance to the sepulchre started of itself to roll and gave way to the side, and the sepulchre was opened, and both the young men entered in. When now those soldiers saw this, they awakened the centurion and the elders—for they also were there to assist at the watch. And whilst they were relating what they had seen, they saw again three men come out from the sepulchre, and two of them sustaining the other, and a cross following them, and the heads of the two reaching to heaven, but that of him who was led of them by the hand overpassing the heavens.[9]

Suppose that in some miraculous way this account were irrefutably established as being, not a second-century rehash of the gospel stories padded out with a mixture of dubious theology and historical romance, but sober eye-witness information. Would it even then be the *resurrection* it was describing? The coming to life again of a dead body and its disappearance from human view is amazing, but it is not resurrection. What can be *seen* is history; but resurrection belongs to the realm of interpretation, of what is not seen and cannot be seen. Resurrection is something to do with the action of God. When it takes place, it may have certain historical concomitants (such as appearances, or an empty tomb) and it will leave its mark on history. But in itself, of its own essential nature, it remains unamenable to historical verification or falsification. The most the historian can do when presented with the external facts—even if they were facts as breath-takingly direct as those of the *Gospel of Peter*—is to say 'this is a significant occurrence and has certain repercussions on the course of subsequent events'; but he is stepping outside his competence as an historian if he says anything about whether or not the event in question is or is not a divine intervention into human affairs, and what its significance must be in relation to God. This is the business of the theologian and calls for the affirmations of faith. These affirmations, like the disclosures of the late Bishop Ian Ramsey, may be evoked by the facts which led up to the situation of disclosure, but they are not logically dependent on them. A logical argument cannot produce material which is not inherent in the premises. You cannot prove a theological point from historical premises. You cannot start with empirical, this-worldly, historical facts and end by proving the resurrection. All you can end with is another empirical, this-worldly, historical conclusion; for example, the conclusion that what happened to Jesus was very similar to the events which modern parapsychologists investigate.

It is, therefore, still our business to look at the events which surrounded the resurrection and to decide what we ought to make of them; and it is still inescapably a matter for faith if we make of them what the gospel-writers and the earliest

Christians did. But the faith which is involved is faith in God and not faith in the resurrection. If the God of the Christians seems to you to be a credible God, then you will interpret what you know of the events surrounding the resurrection in ways which involve the action of God in human destiny, and you will be able to draw from it conclusions which are relevant to your expectations of what might happen to you at the end of your earthly life. That is what we shall be attempting in the remaining chapters of this book.

We have spoken of the relation of historical facts to the resurrection and we have seen that historical research can never lead us by a logically irrefragable path into resurrection-belief. That does not mean that historical research is *irrelevant* to resurrection-belief. The resurrection is a great deal more than the disappearance of a body or appearances to survivors, but it is accompanied by certain marks which it leaves upon history, and the nature of the mark that it leaves upon the physical world *is* important to faith. Different readings of history with different degrees of scepticism about the reliability of the primary data result in different assessments of what that mark consists of. Some people believe it was the mark of an empty tomb; others that it was simply a series of appearances and that the bones of Jesus lie buried somewhere in Palestine; others again, that it was nothing but a conviction in the minds of the disciples. All Christians, to *be* Christians, must believe in the resurrection; but different beliefs about the mark left behind by the resurrection will lead to vastly different theologies about it.

Some Christians believe that there was absolutely nothing factually or empirically observable in the physical realm when Jesus rose. He rose in a purely spiritual sense. His body, like John Brown's, lay a-mouldering in the grave, but his soul goes marching on. For them, 'resurrection' is an event in the spiritual realm only, and their theology tends to lay stress on the element of faith in the preached word and the change effected in a person's life by a changed attitude of mind. If I may speak personally, I must confess that I find a 'reductionist' view like this difficult to reconcile with a belief in the real power of God in a real world. If the only thing that happened at the time of the Easter events was that the disciples came to a fresh realisation that Jesus was still alive and active in some spiritual domain, I want to know how this can be distinguished from a humanly self-generated piece of wishful but false thinking. It speaks to me of human convictions rather than of divine action; and however profoundly a man may be convinced, he is still capable of being in error.

The more traditional kind of Christian (and it is with this camp that I must align myself) will believe that although it is no longer empirically verifiable or historically provable without doubt, nevertheless there *was* some physical change in the Universe at the moment of Christ's resurrection. He will believe that whatever it was that the disciples saw—whether a physical body capable of being photographed, or some kind of quasi-material ectoplasmic mist conglomerating into visible form, or the externalisation of a telepathic message in the form of a shared hallucination—this was not simply the concomitant of an internally reached conviction on the part of the disciples, but a genuine communication between the followers of Jesus and their living Lord, whose mission had not been defeated even by the fact of his death. Clearly, this will lead to a very different kind of theology from that outlined in the previous paragraph, for it will be a theology which has to take seriously the questions of who Jesus is, what he did (or what God did with him) at the resurrection, and why this affects the destiny or expectations of ourselves.

Historical research, therefore, is not irrelevant. But the task of historical reconstruction (in the sense of providing a chronological account of 'what really happened') is, as we have seen, hopeless. Resurrection and history belong to two separate compartments (even if they are inter-connecting), and we do not persuade people to believe in the resurrection on historical grounds. We persuade them by talking about God and what he did in Jesus of Nazareth; we persuade them by showing them that this Jesus is still alive today. 'In the final resort Christians believe in the risen Lord, and only by implication in the resurrection.'[10]

7 Adam's Easter

IN Chapter 4 we discussed the resurrection as a phenomenon such as we might study by the methods of historical research or parapsychology, and the results of our investigation were somewhat meagre. In Chapter 6 we looked at the resurrection again, this time from the perspective of a belief in God and the possibility of his acting in history and the affairs of men. Within that perspective, his resurrection began to look more credible.

It is now time to ask what necessary and logical connection this has with *us*. Even if we grant that Jesus was raised, is that any guarantee that *we* shall be? Jesus had a special status as the Messiah. Maybe that special status made him unique in such a way that his resurrection is the first and last and only case of an event which will never be repeated. Is it proper to move from the resurrection of Jesus to our own resurrection? If so, how is it to be done? Jesus had his Easter, but do we sons of Adam have one too?

Let us be clear first what it is we are discussing. Our subject is not immortality; it is resurrection.[1] Immortality is what Socrates was talking about as he calmly drank the cup of hemlock (see pp. 12–13); the mortal part of man succumbing to the approach of death and the immortal part slipping away unscathed because it is inherently incapable of being touched by death. Immortality is the doctrine that there is something intrinsic in man *as* man, in humanity *as* humanity, in Adam *as* Adam, over which death has no power; so that death is not to be feared or even taken seriously.

The New Testament knows nothing of this. Death is real. It is man's ultimate enemy (1 Cor. 15.26) with a power and a sting (1 Cor. 15.55) that makes every man recoil from it in horror as Christ recoiled in Gethsemane, when he offered up prayers and petitions with loud cries and tears (Heb. 5.7). Man does not pass through death as though it did not really exist. All men die; death is real and to be feared. We are not naturally immortal; only God possesses immortality as of right (1 Tim. 6.16). Or perhaps we should more correctly say that there *is* a natural immortality, but it is the immortality of She'ol, which is more of a curse than a blessing.[2] If this is the only immortality Adam has, it is hardly worth dignifying with the name.

The myth of the Garden of Eden makes the same point. It is not true (as many people are wont to think) that this story shows man—Adam—as a being originally possessed of immortality but tricked out of it by the wiles of the devil. It was not immortality that Adam lost in Eden. He was mortal all along. After he had stolen the fruit of the Tree of Knowledge, he was sent out of the garden to prevent him from taking the next step and *becoming* immortal by stealing the fruit of the Tree of Life.[3] The myth points out that man as a human being is not and has never been immortal. Death has dominion over him and its power is absolute.

The faith of the New Testament is that the story of Eden is not the last act of a drama. There *is* a power greater than the power of death. It is the power of God, the power of the resurrection (Phil. 3.10). In this power the ultimate enemy will be destroyed, its sting drawn, its victory snatched away (1 Cor. 15.26,57). That is why we could discuss immortality without a mention of God, but why resurrection presupposes him. Immortality would be man's possession, but resurrection is God's act. Resurrection is God's way of rescuing us from the curse of immortality! When God has acted through a resurrection, the resurrected man *has* immortality, but it is immortality of a vastly different kind from that of She'ol, because it is an immortality in which God has the controlling hand. It is not a natural or automatic immortality, but an immortality brought to light through the gospel (2 Tim. 1.10), a gospel which claims that through the grave and gate of death—a real death, not a charade—God can reverse what is natural to Adam and can clothe with immortality that which is by nature mortal (1 Cor. 15.53). Glory, honour, and immortality can be pursued by those who persist steadily in well-doing, but it is God alone who crowns this persistence with the free gift of eternal life (Rom. 2.7; 6.23).

Resurrection therefore requires a special act of God; it is not something which God built into the natural order of things at the creation. And the Christian believes that resurrection is something which God did for (or to) Jesus and which he can also do for (or to) us. 'God not only raised our Lord from the dead; he will also raise us by his power' (1 Cor. 6.14). Jesus did not raise himself; the New Testament everywhere[4] speaks of 'Jesus whom *God* raised'. The resurrection was not Jesus as man claiming man's rightful heritage of immortality; it was the breaking into this world of the life of the world to come. As God raised Jesus, so will God in Jesus raise us. 'The icon of the resurrection in the Eastern Church', writes Dr Robert Terwilliger,

> is not of Jesus rising from the tomb—which no one witnessed—or of his being seen in the garden. It is the resurrection of the second day, not the third: it is the Christ who has descended into the underworld, grasping Adam by the hand, and pulling Adam up.[5]

This is the same idea as is expressed in an eleventh-century mosaic from St Mark's in Venice, reproduced as plate V of *Liturgy and Society* by A. G. Hebert, and of which Hebert comments:

> 'Christ in his Resurrection tramples the devil under foot, shaking out of his hand the keys of death, and rescues Adam and Eve. These are not two historical individuals; Adam is man, you, I, the person who lives next door'.[6]

This is indeed Adam's Easter. And Adam's Easter is the work of God, not of Adam.

What we have not yet done is to show any necessary connection between the resurrection of Jesus and our own resurrection, although we have hinted (pp. 67–8 above) that the connection will be found only by a consideration of who Jesus is. That needs a book to itself, but we can at least (within the compass of this treatment) show the way in which different beliefs about the nature of Jesus Christ lead to different beliefs about our own resurrection and the way in which it is guaranteed.

We could, for instance, say that Jesus was simply a human being. If so, then his resurrection proves that a human being can survive death. In that case, it does not matter *who* it was who appeared alive after his death, and the resurrection simply takes its place among the data of psychical research—and that a very humble place, because we have seen that there are many much more recent cases of much higher evidential value.

A variant of this is to see Jesus as the supremely good man who remained faithful to death and was rewarded by God with the gift of resurrection, much as the Maccabean martyrs were thought by some to be worthy of a resurrection which would be their reward for their constancy in the face of persecution. That is a Christology which is not without its supporters today,[7] but I do not intend to spend any time on this view, because it is not the view of the New Testament (thank God, because if only the 'unco' guid' have any hope of being raised, we are all men most miserable). The New Testament is clear that—to put it at its lowest—Jesus was somebody more special than that, and that his uniqueness was not a uniqueness of achievement but of very nature.

Is it, then, sufficient to say that Jesus was God? That would at any rate make the resurrection quite understandable. God cannot die, so of course the resurrection must have happened. It would, however, have nothing to say about the destiny of man, because God is God and man is man and although the resurrection could then show that Jesus was the living contemporary of every dying generation, it is of little comfort to us to know that although Jesus lives, we shall not.

But then, 'Jesus is God' is at least an incomplete statement, and at worst heretical.[8] The Christian faith is an incarnational faith, and we cannot properly understand the nexus between Jesus' resurrection and our own unless we take the incarnation into account. As presented in the New Testament (and especially by Paul) it is given in highly mythical language, but if we are to see whether it can be expressed in terms which we can find credible today, we shall first have to set it out 'straight' in New Testament terminology.

Paul[9] believed that Adam was an historical figure. He also believed (to use the language of biology) that acquired characteristics could be inherited. Adam was created good, but sinned. Through his transgression all his progeny share in his fate of death (1 Cor. 15.21 f.; Rom. 5.12) and go to She'ol or Hades. That is the state of unredeemed Adam, and it is our inheritance as Adam's descendants. This, Paul expresses by the term 'in Adam'. Everyone who is 'in Adam', everyone incorporate in Adam, every human being—that is—who is born into this world, has Hades to look forward to as his right by virtue of his birth. This can be described as a state of bondage, and to be released from it we need to return to God. Unfortunately, man cannot do this if he is solely 'in Adam', because Adam's taint has been passed on to him and he is therefore incapable of making his way back to God. Those who live on the level of Adam's nature have their outlook formed by it, and that spells death (Rom. 8.5). Man can only be rescued by an act of resurrection. He needs to come into union or solidarity or incorporation with somebody who has performed a Godward act at least as powerful and fecund as Adam's sinward one. He needs to move from being 'in Adam' to being 'in' that other person. And that other person is Christ. 'If by the wrongdoing of that one man (i.e. Adam) death established its reign, through a single sinner, much more shall those who receive in far greater measure God's grace, and his gift of righteousness, live and reign through the one man, Jesus Christ' (Rom. 5.17). Christ has been raised, and if we are 'in' him, we can be raised from death to life. We are no longer condemned to the desperation of She'ol, but share the same life which he now enjoys, by a resurrection like his (Rom. 6.5).

How do we belong to one or another of these two incorporations?

A man belongs involuntarily in Adam by reason of physical birth, and his condemnation within the covenant of death is not a result of his own sins—he cannot help it. A man becomes in Christ voluntarily through the spiritual birth of baptism, which is a symbolic death and resurrection whereby he changes

allegiance from the covenant of death to the covenant of life.
We 'put off the old man with his doings, and have put on the
new man' (Col. 3.9 f. (AV)) in this rite.

> By baptism we were buried with him, and lay dead, in order
> that, as Christ was raised from the dead in the splendour of
> the Father, so also we might set our feet upon the new path
> of life. For if we have become incorporate with him in a
> death like his, we shall also be one with him in a
> resurrection like his. . . . If we thus died with Christ, we
> believe that we shall also come to life with him. We know
> that Christ, once raised from the dead, is never to die again:
> he is no longer under the dominion of death (Rom.
> 6.4,5,8,9. See also Gal. 2.20).

Those therefore who are 'in' Christ can share in the benefits
of God's act of resurrection. As we can see from the passages
we have quoted, this is something in the present tense as well
as something which has future reference. The man who has
been baptised is incorporate in Christ. It is up to him to
strengthen and mature this incorporation during his earthly life
by living in the Church his body (Eph. 1.22 f.; 1 Cor. 6.15;
12.27), by constant daily companionship with Christ, and by
taking into his Adamic body the eucharistic elements which
are also Christ's body (1 Cor. 10.16 f.). Such a person will find
that 'when anyone is united to Christ, there is a new world; the
old order has gone, and a new order has already begun' (2 Cor.
5.17) and that he has so replaced the old solidarity in Adam
with a solidarity in Christ that when death comes, its power
and sting will have been neutralised (1 Cor. 15.55) and God
will raise him to a resurrection life wherein that
companionship with Christ is continued, deepened, and
extended in another mode of existence. 'We believe that Jesus
died and rose again; and so it will be for those who died as
Christians; God will bring them to life with Jesus' (1 Thess.
4.14). Such people will never be in She'ol because they have
never been cut off from Jesus, and the fact of death is not going
to cut them off from him who triumphed over death (see John
6.54).

We still need to know how it is that Jesus can be this super-

Adamic figure, able to reverse, and more, all that Adam did. The answer is: Only by virtue of the Incarnation. Jesus was born a man, born in Adam, born subject to death and decay. Yet he rendered to God that perfect obedience even unto death which God desires (but has never had) from the sons of Adam, and was therefore able to break in his own person that old covenant of bondage. In Jesus, human nature had done something which human nature had never been able to do before; human nature had received a new potentiality. This was something which could affect all human nature—all sons of Adam. It was not restricted to righteous Noah or circumcised Abraham; Gentiles and sinners were included in the new dispensation, provided they were brought into incorporation with Jesus. If therefore we join ourselves to this son of Adam whose human nature has been resurrected, his actions can avail for us. This is possible for us because we are sons of Adam, incorporate in Adam, and Jesus, like us, is as human as Adam.

The joining is effective as well as possible because this human Jesus *also* shares a nature with the God who raised him and therefore when we are joined with him in his humanity, we can take advantage of the divine power which is his. Since God was in Christ (2 Cor. 5.19) reconciling the world to himself, he enables those who are incorporate in Christ through a shared human nature to share also his divine nature (2 Pet. 1.4) and, with it, its resurrecting power.

> 'The first man, Adam, became an animate being', whereas the last Adam has become a life-giving spirit. ... The first man was made 'of the dust of the earth': the second man is from heaven. ... As we have worn the likeness of the man made of dust, so we shall wear the likeness of the heavenly man (1 Cor. 15.45,47,49).

God became man as never to be unmade more, in order that those who become his through baptism should be lifted to him as never again to sink (compare 1 John 3.2 with 2 Cor. 3.18).

Resurrection is only for the man who is in Christ. If a man's baptism has not been followed by a life in which that potential incorporation has been made real, or if his incorporation has been fitful or half-hearted; if a man has never left his incorporation in Adam either because he has never heard of Christ or because he has rejected what he knew of him; that man's place is in She'ol. Unlike those who are in Christ, 'the rest of men . . . have no hope' (1 Thess. 4.13). Only he who believes in Christ has eternal life (John 3.16; 10.26–8)—and Jas. 2.18 reminds us that belief includes trust, and issues in a life of particular actions. This would be a dismal matter if that were all there was to be said, for which of us could think of himself as so firmly incorporate in Christ as not to be in danger of falling back into that life of Adam which comes so fatally naturally to all of us? Thank God, Jesus has descended even into She'ol (Eph. 4.9 mg; 1 Pet. 3.19–20; 4.6) and even the spirits of those in Adam who are languishing there can hear his voice (John 5.25,28 f.) and are not without hope. He will come to them, and they will see him. It will be a moment of terrifying clarity which will be painful in its self-discovery (Rev. 1.7). *There* is judgement, when a man looks at himself in the light of the clear knowledge of Jesus and sees what he has made of himself and what he has refused to let Jesus make of him, in this world (John 5.22–30). The purpose of this, however, is a purpose of love. It is for purgation, not for punishment or retribution or destruction. Those who hear Christ in She'ol can even there begin their incorporation in him, and though the process may be slow and painful, they can go with him through the healing pains to a state where they can contemplate both themselves and him without the shudder of incongruity which the first sight of his purity wrung from them.

(Whether that is the destiny of all the sons of Adam, or whether there are those who at the sight of Jesus banish themselves to a realm where they are beyond redemption, is another matter, and one which we must take up at a later stage in this book.)

So far we have tried to set the rationale of our existence in a future world and of the significance of Jesus and of the nexus between his resurrection and our hopes, entirely within New Testament categories. They are categories which were obviously satisfactory to the men of the New Testament because they made sense within their cultural, historical and philosophical background. To those of us who live in an entirely different world from the men of the New Testament they may be frankly incredible. We do not believe acquired characteristics can be inherited. We do not find it easy to attach meaning to the concept of Christ's taking upon himself an abstract yet almost hypostasised entity known as 'human nature' whereby he could have power to affect all others who share that nature and become incorporate in him through a sacramental rite.

Yet it is true that this language expressed to Paul a reality, and that if there is anything in what he had to say, it ought to be translatable into terms which carry conviction to those of us who live in a world which has been moulded by a very different set of thought-forms. Paul used the language of myth. He clothed the existential facts of human and Christian experience in mythical terms. He believed that what God did in Jesus he did in potentiality for the whole human race, because he saw in Jesus that essential humanity to which every mortal man is heir; but because 'humanity' was mythically expressed by him in the (supposedly historical) figure of Adam, he had to balance this Adam-figure with the figure of someone comparable to Adam in his scope but capable of reversing what he saw as Adam's curse.

What we need to do is to re-tell what Paul is saying, but without using the myth of Adam. We need to try to answer Leonard Hodgson's famous questions: 'What must the truth have been if it appeared like this to men who thought like that? . . . If the truth about God's revelation in Christ be such that those men saw it and wrote of it like that, what must it be for us?'[10] If we can do that, we are only translating what Paul has to say to us; we are not superseding it. In the following chapters, therefore, we shall attempt to re-express Paul's myth in modern terms. It will take us some time to do so; and we shall need to begin by drawing a picture of what Christians have to say about man's expectations after the end of this life.

8 The life of the world to come

THE first thing to acknowledge about the resurrected life is, in the words of Richard Baxter,[1] that:

> My knowledge of that life is small,
>   The eye of faith is dim;
> But 'tis enough that Christ knows all,
>   And I shall be with him.

In other words, we must be reticent about the details. That we shall be happy and fulfilled has been expressed in many pictorial ways; golden streets, harps, wings, radiance—but these are only analogies and must not be taken for literal descriptions. We cannot be specific. That does not really matter. There is a familiar sermon illustration about a Christian doctor at the bedside of a dying patient who knew he had only a short time to live, and who wanted to be told what exactly was ahead of him. The doctor refused to be drawn, saying that he could not be dogmatic about any of the details. He only knew that his patient was going to be with Christ. The patient complained that so vague an assurance was little comfort, so the doctor whistled softly. At the bedroom door there was a scratching noise, and he opened it. In came his dog, and nuzzled his face into the doctor's hands. The dog had never been in that room before. He knew nothing of what his surroundings were going to be like; but his master was there and was calling him, and that was sufficient reason for him to want to come through the door and into the unknown room, and for him to know that there he would be content.

The Christian will want to exercise a reticence similar to that doctor when asked to give details of the future life. He will simply say that it is a matter of 'things beyond our seeing, things beyond our hearing, things beyond our imagining, all prepared by God for those who love him' (1 Cor. 2.9).

The territory we expect to explore, though we cannot describe it now, is not insignificant, but the very limitations of our present knowledge, our very lack of detail, may—paradoxically enough—commend our description 'in quarters that would reject a more detailed plan of the Promised Land with every fenced city accurately sited'.[2] As a recent writer on parapsychology and mysticism has said:

> What the true nature of the afterlife is we cannot fully grasp; even the most articulate communicators admit that the type of imagery they plant in the mind of the medium is a bare outline of the true experience. And yet the details become progressively less important as one grasps the fact of eternity as a very present state of being for one who is fully awake.[3]

It is unfortunate if we:

> are not able to observe the discretion of the New Testament authors, including St Paul, in this matter; or to be satisfied with the joyful assurance of the Apostle when he says that henceforth death can no longer separate from Christ him who has the Holy Spirit.[4]

At least, however, we can say that it is of the essence rather than of the details of the resurrected life that we shall in it be enjoying the presence of Jesus; but we must not misconceive what this implies. Father Faber, whose sentimental hymns were the joy of an earlier generation, had us singing

> Father of Jesus, love's reward,
>   What rapture will it be,
> Prostrate before thy throne to lie,
>   And gaze and gaze on thee![5]

This seems to promise a deathless eternity of boring inactivity, which might well fill us with horror at the prospect. That is not the right way to think of enjoying the company of Jesus, as an earthly analogy may assure us:

The young man in love cannot imagine anything better or

more wonderful than to be in the company of his beloved. When he is lucky enough to woo and win her and to find within the state of married life that they do indeed make a pair, then he begins to discover that 'being with' his wife includes many things of which he had beforehand only the merest inkling. Sometimes, it is true, they will simply be relaxing together and enjoying being with each other in a companionable silence. At other times they will be talking, discussing, planning. At others they will be doing a multitude of tasks from washing-up and shopping to gardening and decorating. At other times they will be physically separated and getting on with their own work—for the common good—the husband at his job, the wife in her home, or both with the family. Yet they are 'with' each other in *all* this, and if they are happy in their marriage, they will never claim that 'being with' each other is boring.

The analogy can be transferred to the relation between Jesus Christ and the Christian in the life of the next world. What *kind* of activities there may be we do not know. For myself I hope they do not include standing in front of a sea of crystal and throwing golden crowns in or at it, or wearing a white robe and strumming away on a harp. To think so would be to mistake the poetic fancy of one person for the literal destiny of another. If there is any truth in the accounts we have of death-bed visions (see p. 99 below), or in the descriptions which come to us through sensitives,[6] there may be—at any rate in the ante-rooms of paradise—much work to be done by those who have become used to their new state in helping, guiding, and acclimatising those who have only recently passed over, or in facilitating the work of 'faith-healers'. These descriptions may, of course, simply be the speculative work of the sensitive's own sub-conscious, weaving a likely tale which owes more to her own assumptions of what might be supposed to take place than to any objective communications from the next world. All of which we can be *certain* is that the activities of the resurrected in the life of the world to come will be such that we shall thrill to be doing them in the companionship of Christ, whose company we shall find to be the most stimulating and fascinating possible, whether in activity or passivity. Beyond that, we come back to our basic axiom;

Adam's Easter is God's act, not Adam's possession, and God can be trusted. We leave things in his hand, confident that, with our hand in his, we have what is better than light and safer than a known way.

Having said this, a host of questions then run up and clamour to be answered. If heaven is pictured in terms of being with Christ, where is it in relation to this physical universe? We talk glibly about heaven being a state rather than a place, but surely it must be some '*where*'? And what about hell—or purgatory? Are they places, or states? Is there a '*where*' to *them*? Or are they only possibilities or potentialities which are never actualised? Does God send people to heaven or hell? Or do they go there of their own volition? If so, on what sort of grounds is the choice made? Is it only to believers that God grants resurrection? Is there progress or the possibility of repentance and reformation in the next world, or is it a case of 'whether a tree falls south or north, it must lie as it falls'? (Eccles. 11.3) What happens to those who would like to be worthy of heaven but who feel they will never make the grade?—I know that includes me, and there must be many others who feel like that. What about those who have rejected God for wrong reasons—reasons connected with their upbringing or environment or because they were taught about God in a wrong-headed way? What about those who never heard the gospel or who have been brainwashed against it? Are there few that be saved? (Luke 13.23) Or many? Is God like the Deity of Holy Willie's Prayer by Robert Burns?:

> O Thou, that in the Heavens does dwell,
> Wha, as it pleases best Thysel,
> Sends ane to Heaven, an' ten to Hell,
>   A' for Thy glory,
> And no for onie guid or ill
>   They've done before Thee!

And what about those who are not 'saved'? What happens to them? Are they simply annihilated, so that they become as though they had never been? Or do they go to hell? What is hell like? Is it like the place inhabited by the ghost of Hamlet's father—

> confined to fast in fires
> Till the foul crimes done in my days of nature
> Are burnt and purg'd away?[7]

Or is that true only of purgatory—if there is such a place?

Clearly, we are in a morass of questions. Let us first ask the one about where the future life will be lived, and the answers to the others will begin to suggest themselves.

We have all heard that 'there's a home for little children / Above the bright blue sky'.[8] Those lines were taken so surprisingly literally by so many people for so long that when Bishop John Robinson exploded about them in *Honest to God* in 1963, his words came as a rock of offence for many of his readers. Very many people, he wrote, still:

> think of God as in some way 'beyond' outer space. In fact the number of people who instinctively seem to feel that it is no longer possible to believe in God in the space-age shows how crudely physical much of this thinking about a God 'out there' has been. Until the last recesses of the cosmos had been explored or were capable of being explored (by radiotelescope if not by rocketry), it was still possible to locate God mentally in some *terra incognita*.[9]

We now know, of course, that there is such a thing as the 'observable horizon' of the universe beyond which the galaxies are receding from us faster than the speed of light, so that there are places physically existing where we might locate heaven and never be able to be proved wrong. There is, however, no indication that conditions in places there (or even on unobserved planets of stars within our visible horizon) will be physically any different in principle from conditions anywhere else in space-time. Since the conditions we posit of heaven are incompatible with space-time conditions, we soon get into trouble if we think of heaven as locatable in our physical universe. Think of the problems of transport and communication, let alone of accommodation. And what is going to live there (and how) if physical bodies are not? As soon as we begin to ask this sort of question about a heaven in physical space, we realise that they are silly questions which invite comparable answers. We must look elsewhere for heaven.

If heaven is not to be located in outer space, and indeed not in physical space at all, is there any other kind of space in which we could conceive of its being located? The answer is that it is quite possible to have more than one space, and the relation of various spaces to each other must be a matter for examination and discussion. Dr H. H. Price, formerly Professor of Logic at Oxford, has put it in this way:

> If I dream of a tiger, my tiger-image has extension and shape. The dark stripes have spatial relations to the yellow parts, and to each other; the nose has a spatial relation to the tail. Again, the tiger image as a whole may have spatial relations to another image in my dream, for example to an image resembling a palm tree. But suppose we have to ask how far it is from the foot of my bed, whether it is three inches long, or longer, or shorter; is it not obvious that these questions are absurd ones? We cannot answer them, not because we lack the necessary information or find it impracticable to make the necessary measurements, but because the questions themselves have no meaning. In the space of the physical world these images are nowhere at all. But ... there is no *a priori* reason why all extended entities must be in physical space.[10]

Professor Price's analogy is an analogy with an entirely subjective and self-generated dream world, whereas heaven is not like this; but the point which he makes is that physical space is not the only space. We can logically conceive of other spaces which are unconnected with this physical world, or which are linked with it through such entities as the brain or mind of man, which could be thought of as a particularly sensitive mechanism owing much of its peculiar logical and physical status to the fact that it was the meeting point of two or more distinct spaces: the physical continuum of this material world being one of them, and the non-physical space (or spaces) of the next world (or worlds) being other(s).

If this is the case, then a person can be a citizen of both worlds whilst he is 'in the body'. When the material particles which comprise our brains are no longer functioning, the link with the physical world is gone and the person exists entirely within the non-physical space of the other world. He then obeys non-physical laws, and the things that are posited of heaven are possible because the physical constraints which forbid them in this world are no longer operative.

We said a line or two back that the link between the person and the physical world was broken when the brain ceased to function; but we have looked at some evidence (in Chapter 3) which suggests that for some people at least, for some time after their death, the link can be sustained—though in a tenuous way and only by the intermediary of a psychic sensitive.

To think of the 'placing' of heaven (or other non-material worlds or places) in this way is tantamount to saying that heaven is not in outer space but in inner space; or at any rate that it is in *another* space, so that it can be present to the consciousness of the man who has 'passed' from the physical world to that other space, and that the 'passing' does not involve physical movement, but only the alteration of the direction of the consciousness.

So much, then, for the question 'where is heaven?' What does the Christian want to say about the programme of the next world, or its population, or its furniture? What lies behind talk of judgement, purgatory, heaven, or hell? How do we relate this to talk of the next world as a world of companionship with Jesus, which is part of what is implied by Paul's talk of incorporation and of the relation of Adam's Easter to that of Jesus? Another parable or analogy will help to throw light on these questions; but we will make a fresh chapter of it.

9   Judgement, heaven, hell and purgatory

THE analogy we can use in order to introduce our discussion about the next world, and its relation to Jesus, is the analogy of a sherry party. We all know that a sherry party is supposed to be a delightful occasion. What, after all, can be more pleasant than to mill around with a group of intelligent, cultured, like-minded people, talking about this and that, picking up news and views? There is a general feeling of euphoric good-neighbourliness which the drink and the food help to enhance; and everyone enjoys himself.

That, at all events, is the theory. Unfortunately it does not always work out that way in practice. Have you ever groaned to receive an invitation to a particular sherry party because you know too well what is likely to happen? You come into the room. There is nobody there whom you have seen before, except the host who seems to be busy with another group of people; none of them seems to have anything in common with you and you don't know a thing about the subjects you overhear discussed. You get hotter and hotter and feel more and more out of it—until with a sigh of relief you slip away and go home. When you are asked what it was like, and if you are honest, you may well say, 'It was hell.'

Yet you were meant to enjoy it! Everybody else did. Your host was not a sadist who planted you there merely to enjoy your discomfiture. He would probably be genuinely distressed if he discovered what you had been through.

Let us now try to see the life of the world to come in the light of that analogy. If it is to involve the inescapably closer presence of God and the communion or companionship of saints, then those people who prepared themselves for this during their life on earth by cultivating the presence of God and by bending their minds and personalities in his direction are likely to feel at ease in the company, to find a natural affinity there, and to know and be interested in what is going on. It will obviously take some getting used to; there may well be awkward gaffes and strained moments at the start; but it will in the end be heaven because it will be the consummation of what the man has spent all his life looking forward to. On the other hand, to the man who has spent life turning his back on the light, or having no interest in the things of God, or rejecting all the overtures made by God to his soul, that very thing which was heaven to the first person we thought of—the inescapably closer presence of God—will be the hell of the person who is in the party but out of the swim. He has made himself turn what should have been heaven into hell.

Fortunately, that is not the end of it. There is hope. The host meant it to be an enjoyable party. And when the host is God, his wishes will not be ultimately thwarted. Let us change the analogy. Suppose you were to be closeted for all eternity with Wolfgang Amadeus Mozart. If you were fond of music, it would be heaven. If you could not stand music, it would be hell for you—and, we might justifiably imagine, for Mozart as well. The only way of escape would be for Mozart to take you in hand and give you such a musical education as would enable both of you ultimately to appreciate each other's company. It would be painful hard work for you at times. You would probably call it 'purgatory'. But it would be rewarding. You might need only a little teaching, or you might need a great deal; but the better the teacher, the surer the chance of success.

Transfer the picture from Mozart to Christ, and here we have a teacher who cannot fail, a lover whose advances cannot eternally be rejected, who will love and win even if it takes half eternity to do it. How can a God of love who is also a God of power fail to include one single soul within the orbit of his love? How can he rest until God is all and in all? Until, in our earlier analogy, everybody is at the party and everybody is enjoying it? 'We feel', says Professor John Hick in a discussion of this very point:[1]

as we see in the gospels the divine love going to every length to seek and to save those who are lost, that if in the end of the ages any are finally self-excluded from the eternal life and joy of His Kingdom, God will not merely note with satisfaction that the moral accounts are in balance, but that he 'without whom not a sparrow falls' must be eternally sorrowful at the loss of beings who 'are of more value than many sparrows'.

With Professor Hick, I find it impossible to conceive that the God shown to us in the gospels could be satisfied with a consummation which left him with any cause for regret. It may be important to have the moral accounts in balance, with sin duly punished and virtue duly rewarded, but if that is made the determinative principle of the way in which God disposes of human souls, then it is 'a principle that would rule out the heart of the gospel' by excluding 'the great central reality of the Christian faith, which is God's utterly free and miraculously transforming love for His human creatures'. As such it 'is irreparably sub-Christian, and can only be expected to lead to the development of a sub-Christian theology'.[2]

The only solution worthy of the name of Christian is the one which leads us to affirm that in the end all men will be saved and will come to the knowledge and enjoyment of God's love; that every son of Adam will have his Easter by a resurrection from She'ol. If it leads us to difficulties when seen in the light of other doctrines, then it is the other doctrines which need modification. Christ is the second Adam, not the second Noah; he will redeem all mankind, not the righteous only. God cannot create and love human souls and be satisfied to see them eternally unhappy or even eternally annihilated. Love cannot create, and then acquiesce happily in the loss of what it has loved. The soul of man is too precious a thing either to spoil or to do away with.

There does seem to be a fundamental inconsistency in the conception of a God whose purpose in creation includes as so prominent a feature the emergence of personal life capable of response to him, but whose purpose also allows for the utter extinction of those relationships of love, developed so gradually, so profoundly and yet with such tantalizing incompleteness.[3]

We can believe neither in unending torment nor in the destruction of a single human soul without cutting the nerve of our belief in a God of love who is able to carry his love out in action. As Jesus says:

> It is [the Father's] will that I should not lose even one of all that he has given me, but raise them all up on the last day. For it is my Father's will that everyone who looks upon the Son and puts his faith in him shall possess eternal life; and I will raise him up on the last day (John 6.39–40).

This is the answer to our questionings about those who had no proper chance of responding to God on this earth, or those whose wickedness here has revolted us, or those who, like us, feel they have responded very imperfectly to God's love and his call.

We began this chapter with the analogy of a party. Some people will think that it was too trivial an analogy to express the realities of hell, purgatory, or judgement; but Jesus himself used the same analogy in his story about the man without a wedding-garment who was cast into the place of weeping and gnashing of teeth (Matt. 22.11–13). Indeed, our own parable may show us how judgement is of a man's own making. He sees himself for what he is in the presence of God, and this self-realisation must needs be followed by an experience of purgation before he can enjoy the bliss of heaven in its full simplicity.

So far we have been using analogy. It is time now to see whether, without analogy, we can build up a likely picture of our expectations about the next world. The next world will not be a material world. In this world, the stubbornness of matter prevents our desires from automatically fulfilling themselves; but when this recalcitrant constraint no longer lies upon us, what is there to prevent us from doing—and being—just what we want to be? Will not the next world be a world where our desires are sovereign?

This would not necessarily mean that it would be an idyllic

world. I can do no better at this point than to quote at some length from the lecture by Professor H. H. Price to which reference has already been made.[4] He believes that there is a strong case to be made out for supposing that this kind of a next world might be 'too bad to be true' rather than too good.

The world you would experience after death [he writes] would depend upon the kind of person that you are. And if what I have said so far has any sense in it, we can easily conceive that some people's Next Worlds would be much more like purgatories than paradises—and pretty unpleasant purgatories too.

This is because there are *conflicting* desires within the same person. Few people, if any, are completely integrated personalities, though some people come nearer to it than others. And sometimes when a man's desires appear (even to himself) to be more or less harmonious with one another, the appearance is deceptive. His conscious desires do not conflict with one another, or not much; but this harmony has only been achieved at the cost of repression. He has unconscious desires which conflict with the neatly organised pattern of his conscious life. If I was right in suggesting that repression is a biological phenomenon, if the 'threshold' between conscious and unconscious no longer operates in a disembodied state, or operates much less effectively, this seeming harmony will vanish after the man is dead. To use scriptural language, the secrets of his heart will be revealed—at any rate to himself. These formerly repressed desires will manifest themselves by appropriate images, and these images might be exceedingly horrifying—as some dream-images are in this present life, and for the same reason. True enough, they will be 'wish-fulfilment' images, like everything else that he experiences in the Next World as I am conceiving it. But the wishes they fulfil will conflict with other wishes which he also has. And the emotional state which results might be worse than the worst nightmare; worse, because the dreamer cannot wake up from it. For example, in his after-death dream world he finds himself doing appallingly cruel actions. He never did them in his earthly life. Yet the desire to do them was there, even though repressed and unacknowledged. And now the lid is off, and this cruel desire fulfils itself by creating appropriate images. But unfortunately for his comfort, he has benevolent desires as well, perhaps quite strong ones; and so he is distressed and even horrified by these images, even though there is also a sense in which they are just the ones he wanted. Of course his benevolent desires too may be expected to manifest themselves by appropriate wish-fulfilment images. But because there is this conflict in his nature, they will not wholly satisfy him either. There will be something in him which rejects them as tedious and insipid. It is a question of the point of view, if one cares to put it so. Suppose a person has two conflicting desires A and B. Then from the point of view of desire A, the images which fulfil desire B will be unsatisfying, or unpleasant, or even horrifying; and *vice versa* from the point of view of desire B. And unfortunately, both points of view belong to the same person. He occupies both of them at once.

This is not all. If psycho-analysts are right, there is such a thing as a desire to be punished. Most people, we are told, have guilt-feelings which are more or less repressed; we have desires, unacknowledged or only half-acknowledged, to suffer for the wrongs we have done. These desires too will have their way in the Next World, if my picture of it is right, and will manifest themselves by images which fulfil them. It is not a very pleasant prospect, and I need not elaborate it. But it looks as if everyone would experience an image-purgatory which exactly suits him. It is true that his unpleasant experiences would not literally be punishments, any more than terrifying dreams are in this present life. They would not be inflicted upon him by any external judge; though, of course, if we are Theists, we shall hold that the laws of nature, in other worlds as in this one, are in the end dependent on the will of a Divine Creator. Each man's purgatory would be just the automatic consequence of his own desires; if you like, he would punish himself by having just those images which his own good-feelings demand. But, if there is any consolation in it, he would have these unpleasant experiences because he *wanted* to have them; exceedingly unpleasant as they might be, there would still be something in him which was satisfied by them.

Professor Price, of course, in this lecture was speaking as a philosopher, rather than as a Christian, and was making out a case for what might be likely to happen to our selves after death, if there were to be no other influence upon us but our own desires and character, and if the repressive effect which our conscious mind has upon our unconscious were to be relaxed after the death of our bodies.[5] He goes on to admit that

it is perfectly possible to desire that one's character should be different, perhaps very different, from what it is at present. This is what philosophers call a 'second-order' desire, a desire that some of one's own desires should be altered ... But these 'second-order' desires—desires to alter one's own character—are seldom effective immediately; and even when they appear to be, as in some cases of religious conversion, there has probably been a long period of subconscious or unconscious preparation first. To be effective, desires of this sort must occur again and again. ... In the short run, a man's permanent and habitual desires are something 'given', which he must accept and put up with as best he can, even though in the very long run they are alterable.

Now in the next life, according to my picture of it, it would be these permanent and habitual desires which would determine the nature of the world in which a person has to live. ... Yet he may very well dislike having the sort of character he does have.

This is a non-theistic way of saying that judgement comes to a man, not as an external *fiat* of a God who stands outside a man and tells him whether he is destined for heaven or hell, but as a self-realisation when masks and pretences and repressions fall away and the man comes to know what he has made his character become. Hell, too, is not some place to which God consigns reluctant sinners, but is the state in which that self-realisation becomes effective and a man sees just how terrifying is that naked character, just how tantalising are those desires, just how stultifying those wishes, which determined his course upon earth.

It is the 'second-order' desires to which Professor Price refers us, wherein hope lies; but there is only hope in them for the Christian. The Christian knows the hopelessness of 'second-order' desires when made by the natural man. Paul lamented that fact. 'What I do is not what I want to do, but what I detest. ... The good which I want to do, I fail to do; but what I do is the wrong which is against my will' (Rom. 7.15,19). There is no hope in the solidarity of Adam. Thank God there is an alternative: 'who is there to rescue me out of this body doomed to death? God alone, through Jesus Christ our Lord!' (Rom. 7.24–5). With the help of God, in the solidarity of Christ, the natural man is capable of conversion. The Christian therefore believes, not in a continuance of the helpless moral struggle of unassisted man, but in a confrontation of Adam with Christ, and in the assistance which Christ can bring to the reformation even of the most hardened character. He has seen it happen on earth (he may even have known it happen to him) and he will not therefore expect it to be impossible for any man. He will not expect it to be either instantaneous or painless; but he will know that it *can* be done.

Some people are so impressed by the long and arduous struggle which is necessary before 'second-order' desires can be made effective that they believe it is necessary to experience a succession of earthly lives during which a man's salvation can be steadily won. Theories of reincarnation may have arisen partly for this reason and partly to explain the manifest inequalities within the human race: why are some people more highly born than others, or cleverer, or in better health? Why do some people find it easier to believe in God, or to live the moral life, than do others? If this life is only one of a great series of reincarnations, then we can blame our misfortunes onto the sins of our previous incarnation, and work hard in our present one so as to ensure an easier placement in the next. So stated, there are obvious attractions in the philosophy, and it clears God of accusations of partiality.

There are, however, objections to counterbalance the

attractions. For one thing, if there is an eternity of next world ahead of us, there is no *need* to come back to this one in order to find time to make repentance effective in the remoulding of character. For another, it is hard to see what exactly is meant by reincarnation, unless it be that there is an entity (call it 'soul' or call it what you will) which may attach itself successively to a series of earthly bodies, and yet which retains no memory of itself in its former habitations. It is this total amnesia for earlier incarnations which makes the doctrine particularly puzzling. If a person cannot remember anything of his former life, and is not even given a continuity of physical body wherewith to establish his continuing self-identity through his various incarnations, then wherein can that continuing self-identity reside?[6] The doctrine has no meaning, except the totally unverifiable meaning which attaches to the concept of 'soul' once that concept has been set loose from any connection with self-consciousness: and that is a very doubtful meaning.

'But', it will be argued, 'we do from time to time come across cases in which a person *does* claim to have remembered something of a previous incarnation.' This is true. Occasionally there is the phenomenon of *déjà vu*, where a person comes to a place he has never visited before, and has the strong feeling that he has been there (or lived there) at some other time, and may even be able to say correctly what is around the unseen corner. In other cases, a person may claim affinity with a family he has previously had nothing to do with, and know things about their family history which he attributes to having been a member of that family in a former generation; or there may be people who in trance or by automatic writing claim to have uncovered facts about their earlier existence, sometimes centuries ago. Occasionally a child may show awareness of events he could not otherwise have known about, and the adults around him may realise that what the child is talking about is uncannily like the memories they would have expected to encounter in some deceased adult.[7] These are certainly cases suggestive of reincarnation, but (like so many of the data of psychical research) they do not *need* to be taken at their face value. Often, either the historical allusions are unverifiable, or they are the common property of anyone of average knowledge, or they are generalities; or the information about the other family may have been obtained through telepathy and 'dressed up' as a message about reincarnation; or a 'control' (see p. 27) of the psychic sensitive may be pretending to be a former incarnation of the sensitive herself. *Déjà vu* may be what it feels like to have a precognitive vision of a place at subconscious level, and to be reminded of it as the precognition is coming true; what Professor Chari calls 'telepathic paramnesia'[8] by which term he means a pseudo-recognition of the place or person caused by a previous and unconsciously perceived telepathic message which wells up into the consciousness to cause this *fausse reconnaissance*.

What is also significant is that cases like this which come to our notice are rare and sporadic occurrences. If there is such a thing as reincarnation, then either it applies to a minuscule fraction of one per cent of the population, or their own former incarnations are totally indetectable by the vast mass of people. In the former case, it is unlikely to concern us personally, and in the latter, it is hard (as has already been said) to attribute much meaning to the claim.

For all these reasons, I do not think reincarnation is a serious contender for our attention as we seek to chart our expectations for a future life. We come back to the position we were maintaining a few pages back, which is that there is such a thing after this one earthly life as judgement and purgatory, but that it is hard to maintain that God's love would ultimately be defeated by any human being.

What may we expect the passage through death to be like? There are three areas in which clues towards an answer to this question may be found; out-of-the-body experiences, death-bed visions, and the statements of sensitives. We need to be especially cautious when assessing this evidence, because we have already seen that it may be interpreted in more than one way. It is also dangerous to generalise when individuals may have their own unique experiences. Nevertheless, with these *caveats*, we find that these three lines of approach tell us things about our likely *post-mortem* expectations which are not incompatible with Christian teaching and may be accepted as possible even if not provable.

Out-of-the-body-experiences (see above, pp. 32–7) show that self-consciousness may continue even when the physical body is comatose or in a highly shocked state. This consciousness seems to the percipient to be heightened in quality the more severely the body is under par.[9] There is a sensation of freedom, though the link with the physical body is symbolised in many cases by a cord joining it to the centre of apparent consciousness and it is felt that the cord would break at the moment of death. Out-of-the-body experiences have taken place during brief periods of clinical death from which the body has been resuscitated by the doctors. By extrapolation it seems possible that the first moments of *post-mortem* experience may be similar to what we read in these accounts.

Death-bed visions are less frequent now than they used to be. The classic collection of cases is that by Sir William Barrett (*Death-Bed Visions*, Methuen, 1926), yet the subject is not so much as mentioned in John Hinton's recent (1967; [2]1972) Pelican book entitled *Dying*. Perhaps this is because we are no longer in an age of faith and therefore nobody who is dying expects to be greeted by his departed friends and relations. Perhaps it is because few people nowadays, when they die, know that they are dying. It remains true that there are many well-authenticated cases (mostly from previous generations) in which the dying have had visions of the departed 'coming to fetch them home'. The more significant are cases of children, who will not have been told to expect this to happen; or cases in which the dying person did not know that the person he saw in his vision was already dead. Here is a case which combines the two:[10]

Two brothers, Harry (aged 4) and David (aged 3) died of scarlet fever; Harry on 2 November 1870 and David on the following day, fourteen miles away. 'About an hour before [his] death, [David] sat up in bed, and pointing to the bottom of the bed said distinctly, "There is little Harry calling to me". . . . Care was taken to keep David from knowing that Harry was dead and [the informant] feels sure that David did not know it. . . . The boy was not delirious at the time.'

We could quote many such cases; from them it seems that it

is quite common for the dying to be welcomed and helped through their transition by those who have undergone the experience themselves previously.

Finally, the statements of sensitives.[11] They may be optimistic wish-fulfilment, but there is a consistency in many of them which may indicate that there is an objective basis behind them. Many of them tell of an experience of judgement after death[12] in which the person sees the truth and effects of his earthly acts and dispositions. What is particularly interesting about the immediate *post-mortem* state is that if a person has suffered a sudden or violent death, or if he comes to his death quite unprepared for it, he may regain his consciousness in the next world and be at first unaware that he has died—in much the same way as we frequently are unaware in our dreams of the fact that we are dreaming.[13] We have already drawn the contrast between the Victorian death-bed and the conspiracy of silence which characterises dying today. It may well be one result of this contemporary practice that people wake up from their death in a confused and disoriented state. If, on the other hand, a man comes through death conscious of his unity with Christ and prepared for 'The Supreme Adventure', he can begin his new life immediately, without that sense of lostness which comes through in so many transcripts of séances. As he wakes up, it will be his solidarity in Christ which means most to him, and it is in terms of *that* relationship that the direction of his future pilgrimage will immediately be determined. He will know the direction in which he wants to move; he will know what to do when his unregenerate desires try to get the better of him; he will know how to make his 'second-order' desires effective, because he has done the same sort of thing, and relied upon the same Source of help, in his incarnate life.

The man who has not known Christ in this way on earth has a much longer and a much more sombre future ahead of him before the redemptive process can take hold of him. He has to dive much further into the hell he has prepared for himself before he clutches at the redemptive resurrection which Christ offers him, because resurrection, unlike immortality, is not automatic. A man has to want it; he has to desire that Christ should raise him before the power of God's resurrecting act can begin to be effective upon him.

This means that hell is real, and we are to fear not only hell, but the one who has power to cast into hell (Matt. 10.28; Luke 12.5)—which is not God, but the devil (or, if you so prefer it, the demonic powers, or that aspect of one's self which is opposed to the resurrecting love of God). Hell can be symbolised in physical terms as a fire (Mark 9.48), but it is better described simply in terms of the mental anguish of wailing and grinding of teeth.[14] If it is a punishment (Matt. 25.46) it is as much self-inflicted as sent by God; if a destruction[15] we know that God is able to create and even to re-create; and much of what causes hell needs to be destroyed if the essential self is to be saved 'as one might from a fire' (1 Cor. 3.15). Granted this, I still cannot doubt that God is able to save souls even from hell, unless I also doubt the completeness and effectiveness of his love. To those who say that to jettison the doctrine of everlasting torment is to cut the nerve of moral or missionary endeavour, I can only say that if hell is such as I have described it, then even though it is a state from which God will ultimately resurrect every human being, the suffering it involves is the kind that will lead any reasonable man to live the sort of life which avoids it, and to urge his fellow men in the same direction.

In any case, to try to justify a doctrine of eternal torment because it is a strong inducement to moral striving or missionary endeavour, is an unworthy procedure, which may prove to be self-defeating. The fear of hell is not the same as the love of God, and if our main motive for living the Christian life is the purely prudential one of saving ourselves future discomfort, we are clearly wrapped up in selfish considerations and sadly in need of redemption. Paul referred scornfully to those who thought it wise to sin because they were thereby giving God's grace the greater chance of abounding (Rom. 6.1); the same attitude is appropriate to the man who tells us that it is safe to neglect or reject God in this life because he is bound in any case to save us in a future one. This doctrine of universalism is only an invitation to licentiousness to the man who is already far distant from the mind of Christ.

> My God, I love thee; not because
>   I hope for heaven thereby,
> Nor yet because who love thee not
>   Are lost eternally.[16]

Only the man who is lost in God's love will receive heaven or escape hell and, for him, self-interest has ceased to count. There is a real choice before us in this world, and it is a choice of momentous consequence. It is the choice of incorporation into Christ or of remaining within the old Adam. A great deal of the teaching of Christ puts the starkness of that choice before us. We can try to avoid it by putting questions about the fate of other people—'Sir, are only a few to be saved?' (Luke 13.23); but Jesus will refuse to answer such questions. He will only say to use, 'Struggle to get in through the narrow door' (Luke 13.24). It was the same in his final encounter with Peter. Peter was inquisitive about the fate of another disciple. The only answer to him (and the only answer to us) is 'What is it to you? Follow me' (John 21.22). Our question should not be, 'what about the others?', but 'what about me? Am I living now so as to make God's presence heaven? or hell? or purgatory?' That is a question with very practical consequences for our life here, as well as one with eternal reference.

10 Eternal life

EACH of us has his own favourite anthology of 'worst hymns'. Pride of place in mine is given to one published by Fanny Humphreys (later to become Mrs C. F. Alexander) in 1848. Some of her hymns are among the best-loved in the English language—who would let Passiontide or Good Friday go by without 'There is a green hill'?—but she could at times sink to real depths. In the Standard Edition of *Hymns Ancient and Modern*, as No. 575, you will find the following:

> Within the churchyard, side by side,
>   Are many long low graves;
> And some have stones set over them,
>   On some the green grass waves.

The hymn goes on to tell us that 'Full many a little Christian child, / Woman, and man, lies there'; but that they do not hear or see us, nor can they feel the warmth of the bright sun as we do.

> They do not hear when the great bell
>   Is ringing overhead;
> They cannot rise and come to Church
>   With us, for they are dead.

It is a piece of calamitously miserable doggerel, and not even the assurance that 'we believe a day shall come / When all the dead will rise' is likely to throw off the gloom of the opening verses.

Admittedly, Mrs Alexander was writing, in *Hymns for Little Children*, in an age of high infant mortality, and admittedly her verse is simple and direct; but its very directness only serves to accentuate our unease as we reflect over the teaching the hymn contains. What are we to believe about our friends in the churchyard? Are they asleep or awake? Are they in a state of disembodied suspended animation waiting for a trumpet to wake them? Or are they conscious of what goes on in our world? *Can* they rise and come to church with us, though they are dead? Charles Wesley taught us to believe that

> One family, we dwell in him,
>   One Church, above, beneath;
> Though now divided by the stream,
>   The narrow stream of death.[1]

One family; but has part of that family ceased to communicate with the other part? And what is the unseen part of that family doing?

Christian teaching here speaks with a divided voice. The problem is posed by the two adjacent tombstones, one of which reads, 'blessed are the dead who die in the Lord, for they rest from their labours', and the other proclaiming that the departed has been 'called to higher service'.

According to the one strand—the one which Mrs Alexander used—the souls of men pass after death into a waiting state akin to sleep. They remain like that during the whole of the rest of human history, after which 'the trumpet shall sound and the dead shall be raised incorruptible'. But there is another strand which emphasises the communion of saints about which Wesley was writing, and which insists that the parts of the Church divided by that narrow stream of death have a great deal to do with each other during the interim between this life and the final consummation. Both strands can lay claim to biblical evidence. The sleep *motif* comes out in such texts as 1 Thess. 4.14 ('them also which sleep in Jesus') or 1 Cor. 15.51 ('we shall not all sleep, but we shall all be changed'),[2] and the other *motif* in Luke 23.43 ('*today* you shall be with me in Paradise') or Rev. 6.9 (the souls of the martyrs under the altar, continually interceding to God). Indeed, if there is anything in the evidence we surveyed in Chapter 3 above, it is simply untrue that we all have to look forward to a state of unconsciousness immediately after death.

Are the two pictures incompatible? Only if they are taken for literal descriptions of what things are taken to be like, or exact programmes of the events of the next world. This is not what they are. They are analogies, parables, or models—pictures to help us realise part of the truth, illustrations to illuminate a particularly subtle idea which would otherwise be too difficult to grasp. The value of an analogy is that it helps us understand what we do not know by pointing out similarities to the things that we do know. Its danger comes when we mistake an analogy for a literal description and push it to its breaking-point. The classical example is the nature of God. He is beyond human comprehension, so that one way of describing him is to say 'he is not this, he is not that' (as in the first of the Thirty-Nine Articles, 'without body, parts, or passions'). Since this does not greatly help us, and it may result in a mental picture of God as an indeterminate blur, we take the dangerous step of calling him King, Shepherd, Father, Potter; each analogy giving us some insight into his nature, but no one analogy being sufficient in itself, and each analogy needing to be counterbalanced by all the others. Some analogies take us further than others—Father, for instance. Even this cannot be pushed to include sex, so that we cannot properly ask 'If God is our Father, who is our Mother?', or say that the Fatherhood of God makes him essentially male rather than female. What the analogy *does* say is that there are aspects of human fatherhood which give us a valid insight into the nature of God, but that the fullness of Godhead will always be ultimately inexpressible.[3]

The same is true of trying to describe what will happen to us after this life is over. No literal description of it would be intelligible, because *ex hypothesi* it is not like this life here; but to deal with it entirely in terms of negatives is not much help. There are, however, certain things we want to say about it, and these can be said in mythical or analogical form. If the myths or models seem incompatible, it is because they are telling different stories about different aspects of the next life.

The model of sleep, for instance, speaks to us at a number of levels. At the very lowest, we often feel that our life here is something of a battle, and we feel we deserve a rest before things start moving again:

> All I want is a room somewhere
> Far away from the cold night air,
> With one enormous chair—
> Oh, wouldn't it be loverly!

At a higher level, we know that the consummation of heavenly life cannot be a solitary consummation or an individual contemplation. What would heaven be without human companionship? It cannot be completely heaven until all human souls, of all generations, are gathered together as the company of the redeemed. So we posit an interim period for those who have died early in the history of the world, while they wait to be joined by us, without whom their bliss would be incomplete; and during which we in our turn will have to wait for those who follow after; our children and grandchildren.

The incompleteness of a myth like this becomes apparent as soon as we try to press it, or to treat it as other than a partial insight. If it is taken for total truth, we find it gives us comfortless doctrine about our departed loved ones, about whether they are enjoying their new life and adjusting to their new conditions, about whether they are still in touch with us or concerned with what we are doing. The myth of a long sleep followed by an instant transformation does not answer the truth that we know a great deal in each of us which needs purging and purifying and that if we were transformed in an instant to the fullness of consummated eternal life, then we could not remain our real selves. All this shows that there is need of another myth to counterbalance the sleep myth and to witness to truths which the sleep myth cannot contain.

In any case, there are many places even in this sublunary world where *prima facie* we are faced with incompatibilities, and we have need of a wider vision if we are to see the true uniformity behind the apparently incompatible. It is a commonplace of atomic physics that an electron can be described in terms appropriate to its being a particle or in terms of a wave motion. Common sense revolts and says that an entity can be one or other of these, but not both. The scientist replies that he knows this, and that he is saying neither that the electron is a wave or a particle nor that it is both, but only that for certain purposes and in certain experiments he can treat the electron as one or the other, and obtain results consistent with the viewpoint he is adopting. He cannot comprehend the real nature of the electron. It is simply that it is a useful conceptualisation to treat it for some purposes in one way and for other purposes in a different way. Common sense *may* revolt, but we do not get far in understanding atomic physics if we are hidebound by what is conceivable to common sense. The electron's true nature (which is not a phrase the physicist would care to use) transcends both of the incompatible and partial imaginings of it which the wave and particle languages represent. If this is true even of the building-blocks of the material world, it is not unlikely that it can be true in other fields.

This applies *par excellence* to the attempt to describe the conditions of a future world in terms appropriate to a temporal order. When thinking about life in a future state, we shall have to transcend the limitations of temporality; which is part of what is meant by saying that 'with the Lord one day is like a thousand years and a thousand years like one day' (2 Pet. 3.8). The long night-watches pass in a second to a person sound asleep; there is a subjective as well as an objective passage of time, and the two do not always coincide. The flux of clock and calendar belongs to this side of death, and it is not useful to try and imagine the conditions of the next life as though they were the conditions of this one.

What the Christian affirms about the future life is that it is 'eternal'; and it is to a consideration of that word 'eternal' that we now turn. Those who are familiar with the Book of Common Prayer as well as with more recent liturgies will have noticed that there is a change in the words of the Absolution in the service of Holy Communion as between the Prayer Book and Series Two or Three. The words, 'and bring you to everlasting life' have been altered to 'and keep you in life eternal'. This change is deliberate, and draws attention to the distinction between an everlasting life to which we pray to be brought and an eternal life in which we pray—here and now—to be kept. It will soon (I hope) become obvious that we need two different but related adjectives to describe two different but related ideas about life, but I am far from sure that in the English language the words 'everlasting' and 'eternal' are separable enough to do for us. The *Shorter Oxford English Dictionary* gives 'infinite in future duration' as the meaning of both words, though admittedly it does give as one meaning of 'eternal', 'not conditioned by time; ... pertaining to eternal things'. The Burial Office in the Prayer Book clearly treats the two words as synonymous when it speaks of God's 'eternal and everlasting glory' (with no more of a subtle distinction between the two words here than there is half a dozen lines earlier on in the same prayer between 'joy' and 'felicity'). Hopes of finding a distinction fade to vanishing point when we discover that, although the Authorised Version of the Bible uses the phrase 'everlasting life' fifteen times and 'eternal life' exactly twice as often, the original Greek behind both phrases is identical. There is only one exception, and we will come to it in due course.

The best thing, therefore, seems to be to start with no preconceived notions about different kinds of life which may be distinguished by the words 'everlasting' for one kind and 'eternal' for another,[4] but simply to see what the New Testament means by the single Greek phrase *zoé aionios*.

What does this adjective *aionios* mean? It is derived from the noun *aion* which is translated (according to context) 'an age', 'a generation' or 'an epoch'. *Aionios* means 'lasting for an age', 'lasting for an indefinitely long time'. There are plenty of other words in Greek which are near-synonymous with this one, but the special thing about *this* one is that it makes us think about the Divine. Perhaps this was due to the way in which Plato (who appears to have coined the word) used it. In his *Timaeus*,[5] he wrote that the nature of the ever-existent Living Being was *aionios*, 'a character with which it was impossible fully to endow a generated thing'. There is a most instructive double use of the word in Hab. 3.6, where the Greek translation of the Hebrew reads, 'The everlasting hills melted at [God's] everlasting going forth'. The word is turning into a sort of honorific adjective which can suitably be applied to

God, whose everlastingness is like that of the everlasting mountains, only more so.

It was Jesus who gave the word a new twist. He spoke (Matt. 12.32) of the two epochs—this present but passing *aion* and the *aion* to come which God was about to inaugurate. This new idea meant that the word *aionios* which meant 'belonging to an *aion*' and also carried the overtones of 'referring to God', could mean 'belonging to the new *aion* which God is about to bring in'. The word is a remarkably complex and subtle one, and its meaning can shift according to context. Its meaning has a reference to an indefinitely prolonged time, but it also—and by reason of its particular use in the New Testament—makes us think about God.

So then, eternal sin (Mark 3.29) is sin particularly directed against God; eternal punishment (Matt. 25.46) is punishment in which he has a particular hand; eternal life is the life of God's *aion*, life such as God gives. Not that God has nothing to do with common-or-garden sins and punishments; not that the most humdrum kind of life is not a gift from God; but that in using that particular adjective, we wish to stress the dimension which God gives to our thinking about it. The idea of long duration has not entirely disappeared, but it is the idea of quality which has become uppermost.

When, then can we enjoy such life? Here or hereafter? The New Testament does not seem to speak with a single voice. One strand of its teaching shows us life *aionios* as the life of the coming *aion*. God will bring it in, so its coming is assured; but the time for possession of it is not yet. Thus in Luke 18.30, Jesus promises 'in the age to come ... eternal life', and the Epistle to Titus (3.7) gives, as the purpose of the sending of the Spirit, that 'we might in hope become heirs to eternal life'. The other strand which we see especially in the Gospel and First Epistle of St John assures us that life *aionios* is the life of an *aion* which is even now known. 'Anyone who gives heed to what I say', promises Jesus, 'has hold of eternal life, and ... has already passed from death to life' (John 5.24). John reiterates that 'God has given us eternal life' (1 John 5.11). Eternal life is the gift of Jesus Christ (John 10.28) or of God (Rom. 6.23). Eternal life is to know God and Jesus Christ

(John 17.3). It is to share in the life we enter through the sacrament of baptism,[6] the life in which we are nourished in the Eucharist.[7] The commandments of Jesus (John 12.50) and his words (John 6.68) are 'words of eternal life'; which means that they are 'not descriptions of life hereafter but words which are living and effective to create and sustain eternal life'.[8] If eternal life is the life of the coming *aion*, it looks as though we have already 'had a taste of the heavenly gift, and a share in the Holy Spirit, when [we] have experienced the goodness of God's word and the spiritual energies of the age to come'—which is precisely the claim of Heb. 6.4–5. Christ's risen exalted present life *is* the life of the age to come (see pp. 68–9 above), and all who come to faith in him may share it.

There, then, is the paradox. We may at the same time look forward to eternal life and yet possess it. Paul believed that we live now in the betwixt and between, in the 'overlap of the ages' (1 Cor. 10.11; see p. 69 n.8). We have eternal life; we hope for eternal life. We have to become what we are; we have to lay hold of what can be a present possession but one which has not yet come to its consummation.

Our study of this word *aionios* is making us realise that when we are talking about the things of eternity, the things of time such as clocks and calendars are of very limited use. We seem to be cutting adrift from the ideas of temporality. If so, we need to discuss—though heaven knows how superficially—the relations between time and eternity. Perhaps the best brief way of doing so is to quote one great Christian philosopher and one great pre-Christian one and then see how they fit into the witness of the New Testament on this theme, since the New Testament will enable us to take the philosophers with a pinch of Scriptural salt where we suspect they are only speculating.

St Augustine in his *Confessions* wrestled with the problem. The eternity of God transcends time and looks upon the whole of time, as it were, from a timeless vantage-point. Augustine addresses God, who is 'outside time in eternity':

> In eternity nothing moves into the past: all is present. . . . It is in eternity, which is supreme over time because it is a

never-ending present, that you are at once before all past time and after all future time. ... Your years are completely present to you all at once. ... Your today is eternity. ... You made all time; you are before all time.[9]

Augustine's line of thought is traceable back to Plato, who in the *Timaeus* writes of the Demiurge or creator of all things, who:

planned to make as it were a moving likeness of eternity; ... an ever-flowing likeness moving according to number—that to which we have given the name Time. ... 'Was' and 'shall be' are forms of time; we are wrong when we thoughtlessly transfer them to eternal being. ... 'Is' alone really belongs to it.[10]

This idea of eternity as being essentially non-temporality has gained a strong hold on popular expositions of what eternal life may be expected to be like. Can we imagine experience liberated entirely from temporal conditions? John Baillie's justly famous book *And the Life Everlasting*, first published in this country in 1934, made a great deal of the idea of standing, as it were, outside time altogether and being able to perceive (for example) a Mozart symphony as one 'compresent' entity rather than as a succession of notes in time. Lesser expositors have repeated this illustration, and prosaic and non-mystical Christians have as a result found the idea of eternal life a very difficult one to imagine.

I cannot help thinking that the expositors have been making things unnecessarily difficult for the people they are trying to help. The illustration tries to lift us out of our human mode of thinking and to speculate what it must be like to be God; and it does so by using as the basis of its analogy for non-temporality, an art-form whose very essence consists of successiveness in time. No wonder the mind boggles. John Baillie realised what he was doing, for he admitted (pp. 225–6) that

so long ... as the finite spirit remains finite, it must in some degree continue to experience reality under the forms of duration and succession. ... To contemplate the enjoyment by ourselves of an entirely non-successional life would be to claim for ourselves the prerogative of deity.

His imitators have not always heeded his warning.

Such speculations have their roots in Augustine. They do not (I think) have their roots in Plato. They certainly cannot be found in the New Testament. Plato was not trying to assert the non-temporality of an experience of eternity. His sole concern seems to have been to contrast 'the temporal and the eternal orders: the one imperfect and fleeting; the other perfect, permanent, and divine'.[11] And the New Testament, though it speaks a great deal about the eternal and about eternity, nowhere deals in so subtle a philosophical notion as that of the abolition of time. The experience of ecstasy and rapture was known both to the prophets of old and to St Paul (see, for example, 1 Sam. 10.10 and 2 Cor. 12.2–4), and we are free to suppose, if we like, that their experiences included something transcendental in which their consciousness broke loose from the bonds of time. Eternal life, however, is not to be confused with psychedelic experiences. Eternal life is life oriented towards or given by God. The New Testament is concerned with a man's possession of it rather than with his sensations when he has got it. There *is* a quality to eternal life—Jesus came 'that men may have life, and may have it in all its fullness' (John 10.10)—but what matters is the quality of being 'in' the giver of that life, not the concomitant (or, for some people, non-concomitant) sensations. 'We are in him who is real, since we are in his Son Jesus Christ. This is the true God, this is eternal life' (1 John 5.20). Eternal life is not man's prerogative, nor the reward for man's work. It is the free gift of God. 'Sin pays a wage, and the wage is death, but God gives freely, and his gift is eternal life, in union with Christ Jesus our Lord' (Rom. 6.23; see also 1 John 5.11).

That is good news indeed. Everything that is purely natural has been tainted by the Fall and is ultimately unsatisfying. If we were promised eternal life in which God had no necessary part; if we expected a destiny which was tied up with the old unredeemed Adam; what assurance could we have that it would not be just as insecure, just as subject to change and decay, as our natural life? Instead, we trust God in whose gift alone eternal life lies, and we know that what is to come will not be unworthy of his highest promises. We mentioned a few pages back (p. 108) that 'eternal life' and 'everlasting life' in the Authorised Version translated the same Greek phrase in every place but one. The exception is revealing. In 1 Tim. 6.19, the Greek behind the AV mistranslation 'eternal life' is not *zoē aionios*, but *tēs ontōs zós*, 'the life which is really life', 'the life which is life indeed'. That the men of the AV could paraphrase this expression as they did, shows that they knew what 'eternal life' implied.

We have said very little about eternal life which is concrete or specific. All the same, I believe we have said what matters; that is, that it is life in which God has the prime part, and that we enter it because of Jesus Christ and who he is. 'A faith relationship with God through Christ unites a man to the ultimate source of life in a way which death is powerless to destroy.'[12] Therefore if we begin in this life to relish the companionship of Jesus and to develop our sensitivity towards the things of the Spirit, we shall find that the experience of death—traumatic though it is—will be but a step in a continuing pilgrimage. It means that the hope of eternal life is a hope which can to some extent be realised in this present world, and it gives the lie to those who would try and tell us that Christian faith is unworldly escapism.

There is, however, one thing about it in particular which exercises the thought of many people. We are told that we shall still have a body when we experience that part of eternal life which lies beyond the horizon of our present world. How can this be? And what kind of a body shall we have?

11 Bodily resurrection

Where has thou been since I saw thee?
On Ilkley Moor baht 'at.

THE familiar song poses a ticklish theological problem. If you go onto Ilkley Moor without your hat on, you will catch your death of cold and we will have to bury you. The worms will eat you up, the ducks will eat the worms, and we will eat the ducks. The overall result (though at several removes) will be cannibalism—'then we shall all have etten thee'. If a particle from one person's body can eventually form part of another's, to whom is it going to belong on the Day of Resurrection? Does not the whole business show how ridiculous is the Christian doctrine of the resurrection of the body?

The problem is no new one. It worried Athenagoras, one of the early Christian Fathers, who devoted a treatise to the subject in the second century. After quoting all the best medical evidence of his day, he decided that the problem was more apparent than real. If a particle which once formed part of one body was to be eaten by another person, it would either be vomited out as unfit or else pass unchanged through the bowels. There would be no demarcation disputes when the time came for Christians to take their bodies back again.

That the resurrection of the dead would involve the restoration of their physical bodies was for a long time part of Christian orthodoxy, and indeed (see pp. 63–4) may be traced to one strand of Jewish thought arising at about the time of the Maccabean revolt. Tertullian[1] used the sayings of Jesus to the effect that 'the very hairs of your head are all numbered' and that in the next world 'there shall be weeping and gnashing of teeth' to prove that both hair and teeth would be restored in the resurrection. The original form of the Apostles' Creed[2] is 'I believe in . . . the resurrection of the flesh', not '. . . of the body'. George Herbert, the Anglican parson-poet who died in 1633,[3] was just as sure as Athenagoras that the problem of Ilkley Moor would be solved by the Almighty, though he spares us the embarrassing details of the earlier writer:

> What though my body run to dust?
> Faith cleaves unto it, counting ev'ry grain
> With an exact and most particular trust
>   Reserving all for flesh again.

But what if the Christian faith in the resurrection has nothing to do with the questions raised by Ilkley Moor, or organ transplants, or blood transfusions? What if the problem is the result of a misunderstanding—a misunderstanding as fundamental as the one which led the Sadducees to ask Jesus (Matt. 22.23 ff.) about the woman who had seven husbands, and to whom would she belong in the resurrection? It has always seemed strange to me that George Herbert should have held the ideas I have just quoted. Saint Paul clearly expresses the contrary view that flesh and blood cannot inherit the Kingdom of God, but that the relation between our body which runs to dust and the body that shall be, is far from a one-to-one correspondence; and the chapter in which he says this has been read at every burial service conducted according to the rites of the Church of England from 1549 to 1928, and at a good many since then. Let us remind ourselves of what Paul said.

> But, you may ask, how are the dead raised? In what kind of body? How foolish! The seed you sow does not come to life unless it has first died; and what you sow is not the body that shall be, but a naked grain, perhaps of wheat, or of some other kind; and God clothes it with the body of his choice, each seed with its own particular body. . . . So it is with the resurrection of the dead. What is sown in the earth as a perishable thing is raised imperishable. Sown in humiliation, it is raised in glory; sown in weakness, it is raised in power; sown as an animal body, it is raised as a spiritual body. . . . What I mean, my brothers, is this: flesh

and blood can never possess the kingdom of God, and the perishable cannot possess immortality. Listen! I will unfold a mystery: we shall not all die,[4] but we shall all be changed in a flash, in the twinkling of an eye, at the last trumpet-call. For the trumpet will sound, and the dead will rise immortal, and we shall be changed. This perishable being must be clothed with the imperishable, and what is mortal must be clothed with immortality (1 Cor. 15.35–38,42–44a,50–53).

Before we develop the implications of this passage from St Paul, we need to ask why it was that so much of early Christian thought ignored his clear teaching.[5]

The tomb of Jesus was empty. His flesh and his blood had been removed from this earth by the mighty power of God himself. Since 'he who raised the Lord Jesus to life will with Jesus raise us too' (2 Cor. 4.14) and since Jesus was 'the first fruits of the harvest of the dead' (1 Cor. 15.20), it was assumed that our resurrection would be in all points like his. The first to state this unequivocally was Ignatius who spoke of Jesus' being 'in the flesh, even after the Resurrection' and believed that our resurrection would be 'in like fashion'.[6] The same argument is sometimes used today, though it does not always lead to the same conclusions. Professor Lampe employs it in reverse to prove that since we do *not* expect a fleshly resurrection for ourselves, the tomb of Jesus could not have been empty.[7] We should be on our guard against 'theologians' readiness to take general principles and derive—by some logical necessity which may no longer seem either logical or necessary—specific facts' from them.[8] We could just as easily argue that the unique nature of Jesus implies that his resurrection and ours will be radically different. The early Christians felt it important to insist that Christ's fleshly resurrection was the harbinger of our own. They could then maintain that there was something about this grossly physical world of ours which partook of the very stuff of reality. The temptation from surrounding religious philosophies was to interpret the resurrection as the way in which Christ left this irredeemably hopeless and illusory physical world of decay and death in order to escape to a spiritual world with which it had no necessary connection. In fact, the early Church 'never lost its grasp of the biblical understanding of the unity of man. Precisely because of this it laid stress on the resurrection of the flesh to emphasize that it was the whole man that Christ came to save and whom Christ will raise.'[9] There were subsidiary reasons for the rise of the belief in the resurrection of the flesh. Chief among them was the expectation (based upon the twentieth chapter of the Book of the Revelation) that there would be a thousand-year 'first resurrection' of the Christian martyrs to this earth before the final victorious battle over the powers of evil, and the creation of a new heaven and a new earth. Since this first resurrection was to the earth, it must needs be a fleshly one.

This was not Paul's teaching. It was not our *flesh* which he said was to be raised. In several places he contrasts the impermanence of corruptible flesh with eternal life in the spirit (see, for example, Rom. 1.2–4; 1 Cor 5.5; Gal. 6.8). Flesh and blood, as we read in the passage quoted earlier, cannot inherit the Kingdom of God. Our present bodies are but pots of earthenware (2 Cor. 4.7) held in the shackles of mortality (Rom. 8.21) though capable of redemption (Rom. 8.23). When we rise, it will be in another body, whose nature and appearance Paul can only hint at by such adjectives as imperishable, glorious, and spiritual (1 Cor. 15.42–4). Even if this mortal frame of ours were to disappear altogether, we would still have our eternal heavenly body which is awaiting our use (2 Cor. 5.1). All the same, there is continuity between the old body and the new one, otherwise we would not be the same person after death as before.

This relation of continuity is expressed by St Paul in the metaphor of the seed. What we sow is not the plant which comes out of the ground, but a bare seed. God gives this seed a body as it pleases him. This daily miracle of death and resurrection is a parable of the truth. Just as a field of corn is unimaginably different from the grains of wheat that were sown, so our new bodies will be very unlike our present ones. Yet for all that, they will be related to our present ones, even though they have been transformed. The resurrection will involve a transfiguration of the body belonging to our present humble state; it will be given a form like that of Christ's own resplendent body by the very power which enables God to make all things subject to himself (Phil. 3.21). It will be a giving of new life to our mortal bodies (Rom. 8.11), putting over them incorruption and immortality so that they take on a new form. We shall not be so much unclothed as clothed upon when we receive our heavenly bodies; indeed in some sense these bodies are even now being prepared in us, and will be revealed at the moment of death when the flesh sloughs off.[10] The whole marvellous change will take place in the twinkling of an eye at the Day of Resurrection. The same message is given in a different idiom in the epitaph which reads:

> The body of B. Franklin, printer, like the cover of an old book, its contents turned out, and stripped of its lettering and gilding lies here, food for worms. But the work shall not be lost; for it will, as he believed, appear once more in a new and more elegant edition corrected and improved by the Author.[11]

The seed and the fruit; the shrivelled acorn and the mighty oak; the grubby chrysalis and the gorgeous butterfly. God is not conerned, when our body runs to dust, with counting—with an exact and most particular trust—every particle, and reserving it for flesh again. Flesh and blood possess no immortality. Flesh and blood refuse to do so much that we want to do and urge us to do so much that we do not really want to do (Rom. 7.14–24). Instead of flesh and blood, we shall be clothed upon with another body, a body of glory such that eye has not seen nor ear heard nor has it entered into the heart of man to conceive (cf. 1 Cor. 2.9). We shall not be disembodied ghosts in the Life of the World to Come, but the opening of tombs and the reassembly of skeletons 'have nothing to do with the case'.

Clearly the term 'body' is being used more analogically than literally in this context. Clearly, too, we cannot specify the nature and characteristics of the resurrection body from what St Paul tells us. What we *can* do (and will attempt in the remainder of this chapter) is to ask what truths this talk about a bodily resurrection is designed to protect.

The first point to note is that, for Paul, man was not a divisible creature, made up of an uneasy combination of body and soul, or flesh and spirit, or mind and matter. That was the view of Socrates (see above, p. 13), or of the Wisdom of Solomon in our Apocrypha (e.g. 9.15). Paul saw man as a whole being who could be described from several different viewpoints. He therefore does not use the term 'body' to talk about the material part of man as contrasted with the spiritual part. He uses it to describe the whole man under a particular aspect. So, in Paul's usage, 'body' is not 'something external to a man himself, something he *has*. It is what he *is*. Indeed, σῶμα [the Greek word for 'body'] is the nearest equivalent to our word "personality".'[12] Paul in his use of 'body'-language is saying that we cannot regard parts of our humanity as being irrelevant to our resurrection hope.

Nevertheless, we must not press this too far. 'Body' is not just 'personality' in the abstract. A body is the means a man uses to get into touch with his fellow-men. We could not talk to each other in this world without tongues to speak and ears to hear and brains to interpret; we could not even converse in sign language unless we had eyes to see the signs. If we wanted to imagine a solitary heaven, there would be no need to imagine a body;[13] but if we want to share heaven with other people, if it is to be a corporate experience (and notice the metaphor involved in that very word 'corporate'), there must be something to take the place of our present body, wherewith communication can take place. One truth which the doctrine of the resurrection of the body is designed to safeguard is that we shall not be alone in the Life of the World to Come. As Charles Péguy (1873–1914) once remarked, 'What will God say to us if we come to him without the others?' We believe in the Communion of Saints, and it is the Resurrection of the Body which guarantees it for us.

Nevertheless, the body that we shall have is not our earthly body.[14] So the limitations associated with physical bodies will no longer concern us. For instance, we may have wondered how we should be recognised in the next world by various people. I was known to my grandmother as the little boy she used to take out for walks; I am known to my wife as the person she married and shares a life with; possibly in thirty years' time I shall be known to my grandchildren as that old man who is always reminiscing about the good old days of the twentieth century. How shall I be known to all of them when we meet again? The question sets a problem only because of the limitations of a material body, but these limitations are not necessarily going to be carried over to the new body.

Professor H. H. Price's article to which we have already referred more than once (see p. 87 n.) tries to envisage[15] a possible existence in which persons could communicate with each other and be said to have 'bodies' without having material organs, and in which such difficulties find a ready answer. He reminds us that, in this present world, we become aware of people and objects because our minds receive a series of sense-impressions. These lead us to believe in the existence of material bodies external to us. In the next world, minds could conceivably communicate with each other by means of telepathic messages. If I received such a message from a friend of mine, my own mind could generate mental images to accompany the message. These images could be identical with the sensations caused on earth by his 'material body' standing in front of me, but in fact their origin would be completely different and they would not be subject to the laws of nature which govern material bodies on this earth. Yet they would be a means of giving a 'body' to my friend, through which he could be recognisable and by which he would be able to communicate with me. Similarly, I should have a 'body' for other people, because they could do the same when they received a telepathic message from me. Different people would be able to see me as clothed in different bodies according to how they knew me in this life, whether as a grandson or a grandfather, for instance.

As for my awareness of my body, all the sense-impressions which I receive on this earth and which lead me to believe I am living in an earthly body, could be replaced by identical but subjectively generated impressions so that I would not be conscious of being discarnate until I began to see what strange and non-physical laws my new 'body' obeyed.[16]

This is, of course, no more than a philosopher's speculation.

It is helpful if it enables us to conceive the possibility of what St Paul asserts. If it makes confusion worse confounded, we are at liberty to ignore it. It is an attempt to show how a person may still be said to have a body, even though he no longer has this present flesh and blood body.

Paul insists that, even if our heavenly body is not this body, it is nonetheless connected with it. We could express this in our contemporary language by saying that both this present body and the body to come are attachable to the same mind; but we have seen that Paul (like many modern philosophers) does not like language which splits the indivisible Self into separable compartments. It might, therefore, be better to say that in this present world our personality has been expressed through a particular assemblage of flesh and blood; and that when the personality loses its connection with the physical brain, it must needs take to itself a means of communication and of self-expression which is compatible with what it has become during its earthly pilgrimage. In other words, there is a difference between the earthly body and the heavenly body; but there is also continuity.

Paul expresses this by the parable of the seed and the fruit. We sow our earthly body and we reap our heavenly one. Or, in a slightly altered metaphor, Paul the tent-maker tells us that we are building up our eternal bodies here and now, so that whatever we do on earth will affect our eternal destiny:

> Though our outward humanity is in decay, yet day by day we are inwardly renewed. ... For we know that if the earthly frame that houses us today should be demolished, we possess a building which God has provided—a house not made by human hands, eternal, and in heaven. In this present body we do indeed groan; we yearn to have our heavenly habitation put on over this one—in the hope that, being thus clothed, we shall not find ourselves naked. ... Rather our desire is to have the new body put on over it, so that our mortal part may be absorbed into life immortal. ... We therefore make it our ambition, wherever we are, here or there, to be acceptable to him. For we must all have our lives laid open before the tribunal of Christ, where each

must receive what is due to him for his conduct in the body, good or bad (2 Cor. 4.16b; 5.1–2,4b,9–10)

This ends up on a challenging and serious note.[17] Are the things we are doing on earth helping us to build a body which we shall find it tolerable to live with? Or do we let our minds dwell on things which are not true and noble, just and pure, lovable and gracious, things which have no excellency and deserve no admiration? (cf. Phil. 4.8). Because, if so, we may well shudder with Hamlet and say:

> ay, there's the rub;
> For in that sleep of death what dreams may come
> When we have shuffled off this mortal coil,
> Must give us pause.[18]

It is (I believe) legitimate to carry that model of seed and fruit so far as to say that if we damage the seed the fruit may fail to appear, or else be a grotesquely warped horror; a thalidomide tragedy rather than a beautiful child. The doctrine of the resurrection of the body, as Paul delineates it, tells us that this earthly body is not to be despised but that what we do in it and with it will determine the shape of our heavenly body. That cuts out alike the exaggerated asceticism of the Indian fakir who attempts to despise his body as something to be transcended if he is to scale the heights of spiritual experience, and the libertinism of the man who believes that, since body and soul are unconnected, he can indulge the body to the limits without eternal consequence. It also tells us that it is not only legitimate but essential to take the body seriously, and that there is a place in this world for Christian involvement in the affairs of men and nations. It provides us with the true relationship between sacred and secular, politics and devotion, temporal and eternal. The eternal perspective provides the reason for the whole way we order our temporal life. Religion is not opium but a spur to Christian action.

12 Communion and fellowship

THE story goes that King James I of England (when he was James VI of Scotland) proposed to solve the problem of what language was spoken in the Garden of Eden. He suggested that a foundling child should be put into the care of a deaf and dumb fishwife and be settled on one of the uninhabited islands in the Firth of Forth. The good citizens of Edinburgh could send out a boat once a week with victuals, and in a few years' time they would be able to see whether or not the lad was speaking pure biblical Hebrew.

Fortunately the experiment was never carried out. We know what the result would have been. The poor child would have grown up as destitute of vocabulary as its foster-mother. Men are made in such a way that they learn from the people around them, and unless a child is surrounded by human company, and taught through human companionship, he can never grow to human maturity. Men need a family to which to belong, a community in which to fit, togetherness to bring out the qualities latent in them. 'As iron sharpens iron, so one man sharpens the wits of another' (Prov. 27.17).

Adam's Easter is God's business, and God will not mock Adam. He will not set in his heart desires that cannot be satisfied; he will not make him in such a way as has to be unmade in the future life. God will not eternally frustrate Adam's desire for companionship, for 'it is not good for the man to be alone' (Gen. 2.18). The Christian cannot believe in a life to come which is an impersonal absorption into the Absolute; his faith includes a belief in the communion—the community, the companionship—of the Saints. The life of the world to come is not a lonely life.

That being so, we realise the continuing importance of the

human ties we make on earth. We are made into ourselves by these ties. What should we be without the love of parents or children, or brothers and sisters, of husband and wife? How can we imagine any kind of heaven for us without those who have made us what we are—without whom life would be empty? How many people have said after their closest friend or relative has died, 'If he has gone to hell, then I would rather be there than heaven'?[1] As a retired clergyman once wrote to me:

> If I can't begin by meeting again those I have loved here I don't *want* to survive death. If we have really grasped the truth of the Incarnation we see that God comes to us in human need and human love. The desire to meet their loved ones in heaven is of the essence of Christians' faith.[2]

If that be so, then heaven cannot be fully perfect until every member of every generation of the human race is within it. Therein lies the tension between the 'already' and the 'not yet' of the enjoyment of the life of heaven. Indeed there are theologians who treat questions about the fate of individuals after death as of minor significance; what really matters is the resurrection of the whole Body of Christ, and it is this which is, for them, the import of language about bodily resurrection.

> The doctrine of the resurrection of the body is the doctrine of the redemption and replacement of one solidarity by another—the body of the old mortality by the Body of Christ. It is an assertion that no individual can be saved apart from the whole. . . . The Christian Gospel is not of the saving of individuals out of nature and history . . . , but the redeeming of all the myriad relationships of existence into a new heaven and a new earth, the City of God, the Body of Christ.

Or again, from the same writer,

> The body represents solidarity; and . . . no one can fully be saved apart from his brother, or indeed apart from the whole of creation.[3]

The 'Body' stands for the corporateness of mankind, and

perfection of resurrection involves completion of the body as a heavenly body. The resurrection of the body presumes the communion of saints. We have already said (see p. 119) something about what this implies in relation to the community life of heaven. We now need to show what practical implications this has for us in respect of relations between ourselves and the departed.

The first thing to say is that these relations *matter*. I could not still be myself if at the moment of death I were to abandon all concern for those who remained on earth. If this is true of the natural man, it is even more true of the Christian, for grace does not supersede nature, but perfects it. The Christian on this earth believes himself to be 'in Christ'; to be a member of Christ's body the Church and a participant in Christ's body the eucharist. He believes the faithful departed to be even more firmly incorporated within that same body. Members of the body on opposite sides of the great divide can continue to love one another. It is not only possible to love Christ whilst still loving other human beings; it is impossible to love him *unless* one loves one's fellow-men (1 John 4.20). 'Many waters cannot quench love' (Song of Solomon 8.7); nor can the narrow black stream of death.

Sometimes, so it would seem, this love is expressed in the desire to continue to send messages, and psychic sensitives are able to keep the link open in a number of ways: trance communications, automatic writing, the consciousness of a continuing presence. Use of such methods should not be condemned out of hand, though, like marriage, they should never be enterprised nor taken in hand unadvisedly, lightly or wantonly, but reverently, discreetly, advisedly, soberly, and in the fear of God, with prayerful preparation. Some people wish to remain in contact with their loved ones in this way, and it may succeed if the departed wish it to. It is not a way I would myself wish to employ, but I cannot automatically condemn those who do. I would only bid them do what they do to the glory of God and under his express protection, taking great care lest they be deceived (for genuine communication is rare, and the will to believe has led many astray), and respecting the needs and wishes of the departed. Eventually the time will come to loosen the ties of this particular link between a soul on earth and a departed spirit, and we need to be sensitive to realise when this time has arrived. We want to communicate with those of our loved ones who wish to; but we do not want to hold them in an earthbound and earth-oriented phase when they need to advance in their new life. 'Do not cling to me', said the risen Jesus to Mary Magdalene, 'for I have not yet ascended' (John 20.17). There will come a time when our departed loved ones say the same words to their importunate friends on earth. Those who feel called to make contact with the departed should never do so without seeking the guidance of an experienced, mature, and balanced spiritual director who will be able to tell when things are getting out of hand (as they sometimes do) and whether the continued use of these methods of communication is doing harm either to us or to our communicators.

There are other ways of maintaining contact with the departed which are, to my mind, not only safer but surer. Through the characteristically Christian action of the eucharist, we can strengthen the links between the man who prays and the man for whom he prays by strengthening our incorporation within that body of which both we and the departed in Christ are alike members. At the altar, we join with angels and archangels and all the company of heaven and, because we are closer to God, we are thereby closer to our loved ones than anywhere else on earth.

The eucharist is not the only Christian method of communion with our loved ones departed. There is a communion in prayer which can either be in association with, or apart from, the eucharist. Here, however, there is a sharp division of opinion amongst Christians. The Creed expresses a belief in the Communion of Saints; but does this communion include a communion in intercessory prayer, and if so, is it a one-way or a two-way communion? In other words, ought we to pray for the departed, and do they pray for us? All Christians are united in believing that it is proper to thank God for his grace shown in the lives of those who have departed this life in his faith and fear, and to praise and thank him for the certainty of their joyful resurrection. The minority of

Christians believe that this is as far as our prayers should go; but the majority would want to do far more than this, and include actual petitions for the departed within their prayers.

The reason for wanting to restrict prayer to thanksgiving and the expression of continued spiritual communion is, to put it in the uncompromising words of the Anglican Book of Homilies of 1563, 'that the soul of man, passing out of the body, goeth straightways either to heaven, or else to hell, whereof the one needeth no prayer, and the other is without redemption'.[4] In other words, a man's fate is sealed by the time of his death. To pray for those in heaven implies that they lack something for which our prayers make request, and to pray for those in hell implies that they can be won back for God. Since neither of these is true according to the theology of those who argue in this way, prayer for the dead is an impropriety. In addition, there is the danger of implying that, if prayer can help the departed, it is safe to sin now and to leave it to our relicts to pray us out of the consequences of our wrong-doing, much as happened in mediaeval times with the cult of chantry chapels. Furthermore, the victory of Christ over death means that the deceased is amply provided for by Christ's powers; he does not *need* the prayers of others. In any case, there is no scriptural warrant for the practice of interceding for the departed, which is a custom which grew up after the New Testament was finished.[5]

Those who have read this book so far will perhaps see the question somewhat differently and approach it with different presuppositions. Some of the arguments in favour of praying for the departed have been expressed as follows:

1 Since it is entirely right and natural to express through prayer our thoughts and wishes and hopes for those on this earth whom we love within the family of God, why should these prayers cease the moment the person for whom they are offered passes through the thin veil which separates us from the more glorious life beyond? Prayer is a spontaneous expression of love and, since we love the departed, we cannot help praying for them. To deny to those of us who are left behind the comfort of sharing our love for the

departed in prayer is to deny a human instinct implanted by
God himself. . . .

2 By praying for the Christian dead, we do not suggest that we
are pleading with a reluctant God to change his mind or to
alter his purpose concerning them. Rather, we express a
simple, trustful confidence in the loving care and mercy of a
heavenly Father. We know that for those who love him he
will do more either than they desire or deserve. . . .

3 Few people would feel that at death they were sufficiently
mature for the direct vision of God or for his immediate
presence; nor would they presume that engrained habits of
sin could be immediately eradicated. To hold that any
Christian, even the most faithful, will be transformed into
immediate perfection at death seems to many people
incredible and verging on magic. It would seem that the
turning of a sinful person—even of a person who desired the
consummation of the vision of God—into the divine likeness
cannot be an instantaneous process if human nature and free
will and the continuity of the individual personality across
the divide of death are to be respected. . . . Prayers for the
development of the departed need not imply any doubt on
our part as to the outcome of their further pilgrimage, as
though they could be assured of salvation at the time of
death and yet lose their way thereafter. They may rather be
prayers for a deepening of character and for a greater
maturity of personality. Nor need prayers for light and peace
imply a present lack. We may always pray for an increase
(or even a continuance) of what is currently being enjoyed by
the people for whom we pray.[6]

For these and other[7] reasons, we must insist that we and the
faithful departed ought to be linked in the fellowship of prayer,
and that this prayer includes prayers of intercession offered by
us on their behalf. In the words of a distinguished Evangelical:

Surely that 'tender bridge' that joins the living and the dead
in Christ is prayer. Mutual intercession is the life-blood of
the fellowship, and what is there in a Christian's death that
can possibly check its flow? To ask for the prayers of others
in this life, and to know that they rely on mine, does not

show any lack of faith in the all-sufficiency of God. Then, in the same faith, let me ask for their prayers still, and offer mine for them, even when death has divided us. They pray for me, I may believe, with clearer understanding, but I for them in ignorance, though still with love. And love, not knowledge, is the substance of prayer.[8]

Love, not knowledge. We do not know what the precise content ought to be of our prayers for the departed, because we do not know the precise conditions under which they are living. Neither do we know precisely what to pray for when we are remembering before God a friend who lives on the opposite side of the world (or whom we see on the opposite side of the breakfast table!). Yet that does not prevent us from praying to God for him. There are always generalised intercessions that we may offer, knowing that, whatever else in specific detail our friend may need, our intercessions cover that and more. So we may pray that God's will may be done in him, or that he may come to know and trust God more fully, or that he may grow in the grace and knowledge of our Lord and Saviour Jesus Christ (the prayer of 2 Pet. 3.18). There are, similarly, generalised intercessions which it is always appropriate to offer on behalf of the departed. If the life of the world to come is a life in which unworthy, discordant and self-centred desires are eradicated and in which the soul, in the closer presence of God, grows in the knowledge and love of him whom it was created to adore, then we are on safe ground if we pray that our departed friends may be conformed more and more to the image of God's Son, that they may grow in the inexhaustible knowledge of his love, and that they may share ever more fully in that peace which passes all understanding.

The traditional prayers for the departed are expressed in such terms as 'Rest eternal grant unto them, O Lord, and let light perpetual shine upon them'. The prayer is not to be taken literally; rest for ever would soon become boring and it is not necessarily enjoyable to live in the glare of sunlight all the time. We are praying in terms of myths, analogies, models. Rest is a synonym for all that is pleasant, and light is a symbol for the presence of God, for what is welcome and joyful and good—the opposite of darkness, which is the symbol of dread, of Satan, of despair, of confusion. So we pray that the departed may grow in the enjoyment of God, and rest in the goodness of Christ. We do not imply, by praying for this, that they are not already enjoying it; we simply acknowledge that this is what is good, and this is our wish for them, and that this can only be granted by God, which is why it is to God that we are addressing our request. Such a prayer, we can be assured, is within God's will for the people we bring before him. Since we believe that hell, though real, is not everlasting, we can pray a prayer in these words for every human being and still not be afraid of praying contrary to God's will.

What about prayers offered by the departed for us? It is reasonable to suppose that they will still want to help those whom they still love. 'Think of all the true hearts who have lived on earth the Christ-life of unselfish helpfulness. Can you imagine them never helping anyone there, where growth in love is God's highest aim for them?'[9] Part of such help will be a help in prayer. When they were on earth, we used to say to them, 'Say a prayer for us' without meaning thereby to take away one jot or tittle from the fact that prayer is offered to God through Jesus alone. We can still say to them, who are closer to Jesus than any of our friends here on earth, 'Say a prayer for us'. I cannot believe that God would ever count that a sin, or that Jesus would be so jealous of his sole prerogatives as to want the departed to stop that exercise of prayer which meant so much to them whilst they were still on this earth.

The same goes for the dead whom we never knew as earthly persons, but with whom we are nonetheless linked in the Body of Christ. There are many people we know who are always finding fresh friends to make and fresh people to help. We cannot suppose the Saints of God to be any less keen to help if they are asked. Admittedly, there is the difficulty of imagining how they might cope with the sheer volume of requests for prayer which come their way, but conditions of time and space and attention are likely to be so radically different in the next world that this problem may be a problem solely of our imagination.

To ask the saints to pray for us, is not likely to infringe the sole rights of Christ.

> Christ's unique kingship is exercised by His bestowal of Himself to His Church. His distinct individuality consists, not in His exclusive possession of what other people cannot have, but in His unique bestowal of what nobody else can give. Can he not therefore give—e.g., prevailing power to the prayers of the Saints?[10]

So we pray (and give honour to Christ by praying) through the saints to him, asking them to intercede with him for us. They will not get between him and us, because it is only in him and through him that the prayer can be offered at all. Indeed, this prayer serves to emphasise and cement the communal nature of the Christian faith, the fact that our relation to Christ is not a solitary and an individual relation, but that we are part of one communion and fellowship wherein we are persuaded that neither death nor life shall be able to separate us from the love of God in Christ Jesus our Lord (cf. Rom. 8.38 f.) and from our communion in his Body. Those who believe in the Communion of Saints should live and pray through Christ in that conviction.

Christians believe in the Communion of saints and in the resurrection to life eternal. This is a faith which has both present significance and future hope. Paul spoke of the body of the life of the world to come as a body of glory, in which we should share the splendour which is Christ's. 'Because there is for us no veil over the face', he wrote (2 Cor. 3.18), 'we all reflect as in a mirror the splendour of the Lord; thus we are transformed into his likeness, from splendour to splendour; such is the influence of the Lord who is Spirit'. The analogy is that of the refiner's fire. He looks into the open furnace and knows that the purifying is complete and the dross all burnt away when he can see his own image reflected in the molten metal. God's discipline of us is for nothing less than that he may be able to look at us and see his own glory reflected. We have 'the gospel of the glory of Christ. ... For the same God who said, "Out of darkness let light shine", has caused his light to shine within us, to give the light of revelation—the revelation of the glory of God in the face of Jesus Christ' (2 Cor. 4.4-6). We are destined for an eternal glory which far outweighs our slight and short-lived troubles (2 Cor. 4.17). We know that eventually we shall be like Christ, for we shall see him as he is (1 John 3.2); we shall share in God's very being (2 Pet. 1.4). This is a doctrine of very practical consequence, because it affects the way in which we live our everyday life and treat our everyday neighbour. C. S. Lewis once gave lyrical expression to this same truth:

> It may be possible for each to think too much of his own potential glory hereafter; it is hardly possible for him to think too often or too deeply about that of his neighbour. The load, or weight, or burden of my neighbour's glory should be laid daily on my back, a load so heavy that only humility can carry it, and the backs of the proud will be broken. ... There are no *ordinary* people. You have never talked to a mere mortal. Nations, cultures, arts, civilizations—these are mortal, and their life is to ours as the life of a gnat. But it is immortals whom we joke with, work with, marry, snub, and exploit. ... Next to the Blessed Sacrament itself, your neighbour is the holiest object presented to your senses. If he is your Christian neighbour he is holy in almost the same way, for in him also Christ *vere latitat*—the glorifier and the glorified, Glory Himself, is truly hidden.[11]

In other words, as C. S. Lewis said at the beginning of that memorable paragraph, 'the cross comes before the crown and tomorrow is a Monday morning'. It is as a Monday morning faith that the faith of the resurrecting God must be held. We have spent a good many pages trying to see what can reasonably be held about our future destiny. It is important to see where we are going, but only if we bring it back from the realm of speculation into that of practical conduct. If resurrection only means that something will happen to us willy-nilly some day, then study of it only serves to gratify curiosity; but if it reacts back on the way we shape our lives in this world, it is indeed a proper subject to discuss. I have tried continually through this book to do two things. The first is to show the link between the empirical evidence of psychical research and the claims of Christian theology, and the second is to show the connection between our beliefs concerning the next world and our conduct in this. I believe I have shown the reasonableness of the Christian claims and the way in which they are supported by such empirical evidence as we have, though the evidence by itself would not take us anything like so far as Christians want to go. But faith is seen to take off from where knowledge leads, and to be going in the same direction. So Christians who hold the resurrection faith may be reasonably sure that they are not pursuing a chimaera. They may also be sure that their faith has practical, everyday, implications. Therefore they make it their aim to live as those who believe and trust in the communion of saints, the forgiveness of sins, and the resurrection to life everlasting, and they pray that God may strengthen this faith and hope in them all the days of this life until he brings them to the life of the world to come.

Notes

CHAPTER 1

[1] See Norman Autton, *The Pastoral Care of the Dying* (SPCK, 1966), pp. 32–8, and J. Hinton, *Dying* (Penguin, [2]1972), p. 78.

[2] *Hamlet*, III. i. 78–82.

[3] See Hinton, *op. cit.*, p. 84. Atheists and committed Christians show less anxiety about impending death than agnostics or nominal churchgoers.

[4] J. B. Priestley, *Over the Long High Wall* (Heinemann, 1972), p. 46.

[5] The ORC's figures are that 39 per cent believe in life after death, 35 per cent do not, and 27 per cent profess not to know. Figures for burial services without religious rites are harder to come by. Dr W.S.F. Pickering ('The Persistence of Rites of Passage', *British Journal of Sociology*, 25(1974), pp. 63–78) admits that 'virtually no sociological studies have been made about burials in contemporary Britain' and hazards the guess that 'virtually 100% of burials are accompanied by a religious ceremony'. That may be true of burials, but he may be overstating the case if one considers cremations as well. During $3\frac{1}{2}$ months of 1974 (and I am grateful to Peter Wyld of the Church of England Enquiry Centre for finding this out for me) out of over 1000 funerals at Golders Green Crematorium, almost exactly 5 per cent were without any religious service. This 5 per cent is probably higher than the national average; at Durham crematorium, for example, out of 431 committals during the fourth quarter of 1974, not a single one was unaccompanied by a minister of religion.

[6] Bede, *A History of the English Church and People*, II. 13 (translated by Leo Sherley-Price: Penguin Classics edition, revised 1968, p. 127). The incident occurred in AD 627.

[7] J. Paterson Smyth, *The Gospel of the Hereafter* (Hodder & Stoughton, 1910), p. 213.

[8] The version is by W. H. Draper (1855–1933) and appears as No. 172 of *Hymns Ancient and Modern Revised*.

[9] *The Song of Brother Sun*, in *English Rime* (1926).

[10] M. L. Haskins, *The Gate of the Year*, quoted in *King George VI to his Peoples* (John Murray, 1952), p. 21. (Christmas Day, 1939).

CHAPTER 2

[1] *AV*. The *NEB* translates 'the harvest of the dead' and 'those who died as

Christians', but the Greek uses the word *koimaomai*, 'I fall asleep, I am asleep'.

² But see also, e.g., Deut. 31.16 and 2 Sam. 7.12 (*AV*). The Hebrew word meaning 'to lie down' is used indiscriminately of sleep, sexual intercourse, and death.

³ 'When my perceptions are removed for any time, as by sound sleep, so long am I insensible of *myself*, and may truly be said not to exist' (David Hume, *A Treatise of Human Nature*(1739), 1.4.6).

⁴ As reported by Plato in *Phaedo*, 106e (trans. B. Jowett, *The Dialogues of Plato* (Clarendon Press) 4th edition, revised 1953). The same idea underlies the 'Wisdom of Solomon' in our *Apocrypha*, which probably dates from about the first century BC. See 9.15, 'a perishable body weighs down the soul', and 15.8, 'this man who ... returns to the place whence he was taken, when the living soul that was lent to him must be repaid'.

⁵ If it does. Some people claim that old age brings to them a sense of rounding-off, of completion, of work done and rest deserved.

⁶ *The Great Mystery of Life Hereafter* (articles reprinted from *The Sunday Times*, January to March 1957), Hodder & Stoughton (1957), pp. 25, 27.

CHAPTER 3

¹ There is a brief discussion entitled 'The evidence of psychical research' in the report of the Archbishops' Commission on Christian Doctrine on *Prayer and the Departed* (SPCK, 1971), pp. 61–6, but the best, the most readable, and the most judicious summary of the evidence in under 20,000 words known to me is to be found in the chapter by Rosalind Heywood which forms pages 219–50 of *Man's Concern with Death*, by Arnold Toynbee and others (Hodder & Stoughton, 1968).

² *A Midsummer Night's Dream*, 5. i. 18–22.

³ G. W. Lambert. 'An Auditory Hallucination Apparently Connected with a Death at a Distance', *Journal* of the SPR, 43(1966), pp. 363–6.

⁴ This would apply, for instance, to the apparition of C. S. Lewis seen by Canon J. B. Phillips and recounted on pp. 88–90 of Canon Phillips's *Ring of Truth* (Hodder & Stoughton, 1967). This case is a cautionary tale; Canon Phillips's recollection was that it happened only a few days after C. S. Lewis's death, and he so told the story. Later correspondence elicited the fact that it took place some months later, not long after Canon Phillips had received a letter reminding him of Lewis's death. (See Andrew Mackenzie and K. M. Goldney, *Journal* of the SPR, 45(1970), pp. 381–91, and M. C. Perry, *ibid.*, 46(1971), pp. 203–5.) One cannot be too careful in checking accounts of allegedly paranormal happenings.

⁵ Rosalind Heywood, 'Apparition of a Dog and its Mistress', *Journal* of the SPR, 39(1958), pp. 240–2.

⁶ Augustine, *de cura pro mortuis*, 11.13, as condensed by G. Zorab in *Journal* of the SPR, 41(1962), p. 410. See also E. R. Dodds, 'Supernormal

Phenomena in Classical Antiquity', *Proceedings* of the SPR, 55(1971), p. 202, where Professor Dodds adds that Augustine, 'with characteristic caution and acumen, warns us against assuming too hastily that the source of the supernormal apprehension in such cases is necessarily the deceased person'. Zorab makes the same observation. See Peter Brown, *Augustine of Hippo* (Faber, 1967), pp. 413–8, on the general subject of Augustine and the paranormal.

[7] *Proceedings* of the SPR, 10(1894).

[8] Hornell Hart *et al.*, *Proceedings* of the SPR, 50(1956), pp. 153–239.

[9] *Journal* of the American SPR, 26, pp. 174–5; quoted by Hornell Hart, *art. cit. supra*, pp. 163–4.

[10] Hornell Hart, *art. cit. supra*, pp. 165, 167.

[11] We say '*her* hand' because the vast majority of sensitives are female, though (for instance) I know one clergyman who regularly practises automatic writing and believes he is thereby in direct touch with his deceased father; for details see C. E. J. Fryer, *A Hand in Dialogue* (Churches' Fellowship for Psychical and Spiritual Studies, 1975).

[12] Playing around with a ouija board may begin as a joke and end in terror, obsession, or mental disturbance. For some reason, it frequently results in messages which foretell disaster or death to one or other of the sitters or to their close friends or relatives. This may be because it is a means whereby the sitter's repressed subconscious is allowed out (and we know what hidden violence lurks even within the meekest of mortals—often *especially* in the meekest of mortals), or it may be because, in the words of Dr Martin Israel, 'not all psychic communication is desirable, especially as it is the more earth-bound type of entity that is most likely to communicate, and to obsess or even to possess the psychic if given the opportunity'. ('The Nearness of God', in *Life, Death and Psychical Research*, edited by J. D. Pearce-Higgins and G. S. Whitby (Rider, 1973), p.261.)

[13] For sound advice, read *Hints on Sitting with Mediums* (SPR, revised edition, 1965).

[14] Quoted by Susy Smith, *The Mediumship of Mrs Leonard* (University Books, New York, 1964), pp. 130–1.

[15] W. H. Salter, *Zoar: The Evidence of Psychical Research Concerning Survival* (Sidgwick & Jackson, 1961), pp. 204, 207. Salter was the husband of Helen Verrall.

[16] We have already (n. 1 above) commended Rosalind Heywood's chapter in *Man's Concern with Death*. Particularly apposite in relation to the cross-correspondences are pp. 235–42.

[17] Garth Moore, *Survival—a Reconsideration* (The Myers Memorial Lecture for 1966, SPR), pp. 14–15.

[18] Paul's phrase—see 2 Cor. 12.2 f.

[19] From a letter in *The Sunday Times*, 25 March 1962; quoted by Rosalind Heywood in *Man's Concern with Death*, by Arnold Toynbee *et al.* (Hodder & Stoughton, 1968), p. 197.

[20] The case was first reported in *To Live Again* by Catherine Marshall, and is summarised by J. D. Pearce-Higgins in *Life, Death and Psychical*

Research, edited by J. D. Pearce-Higgins and G. S. Whitby (Rider, 1973), pp. 229–31, from which source the quotations above are taken.

²¹ G. S. Whitby, *The Modern Churchman*, 16(n.s.) 1972, pp. 80–1.

²² It has occurred—amongst others— to Socrates, Plotinus, Wordsworth, Tennyson, Jung, D. H. Lawrence, Arthur Koestler and Ernest Hemingway. For recent books recounting the personal experiences of those to whom it is habitual, see J. H. M. Whiteman,*The Mystical Life* (Faber, 1961) and Robert A. Monroe, *Journeys out of the Body* (Souvenir Press, 1972). There are useful discussions of the phenomenon by Rosalind Heywood in *Man's Concern with Death*, pp. 185–218 and Professor Sir Cyril Burt in *Psychology and Psychical Research* (The Myers Memorial Lecture for 1968; SPR), pp. 76–90.

²³ Martin Israel in *Life, Death and Psychical Research* (Rider, 1973), edited by J. D. Pearce-Higgins and G. S. Whitby, p. 263.

²⁴ *Journal* of the SPR, 44 (1967), pp. 111–31.

²⁵ R. B. Y. Scott, *The Anchor Bible, Proverbs and Ecclesiastes* (Doubleday, 1965), p. 255. This is the only place in the Old Testament where the Hebrew word for 'rope' is used metaphorically of the cord of life. The *NEB* does use the expression 'thread of life' elsewhere in the Old Testament (e.g. Job 8.13; Prov. 11.7, 23.18, 24.14; Ezek. 37.11), but this comes from an entirely different Hebrew word whose verbal root is associated with the idea of tension or stretching and so comes to mean enduring, waiting for, or hoping. So its normal meaning (e.g. in Ezek. 19.5; Prov. 10.28; Job 4.6) is 'hope', but it can (e.g. in Josh. 2.18,21) be translated 'cord', and there are—as we have seen—places where the *NEB* translators, unlike those of any previous English version, have rendered it 'life-thread' or 'thread of life'. Job 7.6 is especially instructive. The *NEB* text runs 'My days are swifter than a shuttle and come to an end as the thread runs out', but the margin gives the alternative translation, 'My days . . . come to an end without hope'. (I am no Hebraist and gratefully acknowledge my indebtedness to E. W. Heaton in this footnote.)

²⁶ Cyril Burt, *Psychology and Psychical Research* (SPR, 1968), pp. 79f.

²⁷ Dr J. F. McHarg in *Journal* of the SPR, 47(1973), p. 51.

²⁸ Rosalind Heywood in *Man's Concern with Death*, p. 199.

²⁹ Cyril Burt, *op. cit.*, p. 80.

³⁰ Case quoted in Rosalind Heywood, *op. cit.*, p. 199, n. 3.

³¹ See Norman Autton, *Pastoral Care of the Dying* (SPCK,1966), p. 81.

³² The title of a book on psychical research by G. N. M. Tyrrell (Penguin Books, 1947).

³³ *Proceedings* of the SPR, 18(1903), p. 59.

³⁴ See N. O. Jacobsen, *Life Without Death?* (Turnstone, 1974), p. 175. But compare Ian Stevenson in *Journal* of the SPR, 48 (1975), pp. 123f.

CHAPTER 4

¹ Origen, *contra Celsum*, ii 55.

² M. C. Paternoster, *Stronger than Death* (SPCK, 1972), p. 28. Morison's book appeared in 1930.

[3] M. C. Paternoster, *op. cit.*, p. 28.

[4] A. C. Doyle, *The Sign of Four* (his italics).

[5] And I must admit to having been among them; pp. 33–133 of my earlier book *The Easter Enigma* (Faber, 1959) are pure *habeas corpus*.

[6] 1 Cor. 15.5; there is a trace of this tradition in Luke 24.34 and a further one in John 20.2–7.

[7] *The Resurrection of Jesus of Nazareth* (Engl. trans. by Margaret Kohl), SCM Press, 1970, pp. 95–6 (author's italics).

[8] G. Bornkamm, *Jesus of Nazareth* (1963), pp. 182 f.

[9] Mark 16.9–20 is a later addition to the gospel.

[10] C. F. Evans, *Resurrection and the New Testament* (SCM Press, Studies in Biblical Theology, second series, 12(1970), p. 128.

[11] See G. W. E. Nickelsburg, *Resurrection, Immortality, and Eternal Life in Intertestamental Judaism* (OUP, 1972).

[12] C. F. Evans, *op. cit.*, p. 27, pp. 39–40.

[13] It would be wrong to let the reader unfamiliar with current New Testament studies infer from what has been written above that Marxsen and Fuller do not believe in the resurrection. This is far from the truth. Marxsen is a Christian, but he believes that faith should be based on the Jesus who meets us in the preached word, not on such rationalistic and human foundations as the material and tangible and physical evidence of historical research. He writes at the conclusion of his book: 'The believer only radically believes if he believes like Jesus and thinks that, contrary to appearances, God can do *anything*. That is why Jesus makes us free for limitless faith in this world and utter confidence in God for the future' (p. 188). Professor Fuller is also a convinced Christian who urges us to base our preaching, not on what he conceives to be the doubtful and pseudo-historical details of the gospel narratives, but on the central message of the resurrection proclamation and on the present livingness of Jesus.

CHAPTER 5

[1] The title of an article by Professor E. R. Dodds in *Proceedings* of the SPR, 55(1971), pp. 189–237 (which does not even mention the resurrection).

[2] Augustine, *Confessions*, 1.1.

[3] Bishop J. A. Pike with Diane Kennedy, *The Other Side* (W. H. Allen, 1969).

[4] Bishop J. A. Pike, *op. cit.*, pp. 299–300.

[5] Professor Charles Richet, 'The Difficulty of Survival from the Scientific Point of View', *Proceedings* of the SPR, 34(1924), pp. 112–13; his italics.

[6] See H. H. Price, *Essays in the Philosophy of Religion* (OUP, 1972). Chapter 5 (pp. 78–97) is entitled 'Motives for Disbelief in Life after Death', and develops this theme.

CHAPTER 6

[1] C. F. Evans, *op. cit.*, p. 16. See also chapter 5, n. 11 *supra*.

² C. F. Evans, *op. cit.*, p. 16 n. See also Gerald O'Collins, *The Easter Jesus* (Darton, Longman & Todd, 1973), pp. 104–6.

³ C. F. Evans, *op. cit.*, p. 17 n.

⁴ *Book of Common Prayer*, Collect of Trinity 12 (and see also the Collect of Trinity 6).

⁵ John Knox, *Christ and the Hope of Glory* (Abingdon Press, Nashville, Tennessee, 1960), pp. 43–4.

⁶ William Strawson, *Jesus and the Future Life* (Epworth Press, revised edition, 1970), p. 127.

⁷ Gerald O'Collins, *The Easter Jesus* (Darton, Longman & Todd, 1973), p. 31 (his italics).

⁸ See 1 Cor. 10.11. I regret I have forgotten the provenance of this picturesque translation.

⁹ *Gospel of Peter* 9(35)–10(40), from *New Testament Apocrypha* (ed. W. Schneemelcher; trans. and ed. by R. McL. Wilson), Lutterworth Press 1963, vol. 1, pp. 185 ff.

¹⁰ D. H. van Daalen, *The Real Resurrection* (Collins, 1972), pp. 55 ff.

CHAPTER 7

¹ An excellent discussion of the distinctions between the two concepts is to be found in Oscar Cullmann, *Immortality of the Soul or Resurrection of the Dead?: The Witness of the New Testament* (Epworth, 1958).

² See above, p. 61; and compare Maurice Wiles, *The Remaking of Christian Doctrine* (SCM Press, 1974, p. 129): 'If man has an immortal soul, he has it only because God has so created him.' Wiles goes on to say (p. 135): 'if we were concerned with the bare fact of continued existence after death, the language of immortality understood as a gift of God in the order of creation would be fully appropriate. But if we are concerned at the same time with the quality of life, as Christian faith emphatically is, resurrection language is more suitable.'

³ Gen. 3.22. It was Paul who taught that Adam's sin brought death into the world (see p. 77 below); Genesis maintained that it would have come in any case.

⁴ Though see 1 Thess. 4.14a and John 10.17f.

⁵ 'Experiencing the Resurrection', *Christian*, 1:1(1973), p. 20.

⁶ A. G. Hebert, *op. cit.*, (Faber, 1935; paperback, 1961), p. 72.

⁷ See, for example, David Welbourn, *God-Dimensional Man* (Epworth Press, 1972).

⁸ See Nels F. S. Ferré, 'Is the Basis of the World Council Heretical?', *Expository Times*, 74(1962), pp. 66–8 and subsequently *ibid.*, pp. 100–2 and 328.

⁹ The Rabbinic background of Paul's theology is important here, but it would take us too far afield to discuss it. See W. D. Davies, *Paul and Rabbinic Judaism* (SPCK, 1948), especially Chapter 3, 'The Old and the New Humanity: the First and Second Adam' (pp. 36–57).

¹⁰ *For Faith and Freedom* (Blackwell, 1956), I, pp. 87 ff.

CHAPTER 8

[1] 1615–91. Quoted from verse 5 of his hymn 'Lord, it belongs not to my care' (*Hymns Ancient and Modern Revised*, No. 342).

[2] W. H. Salter, *Zoar: The Evidence of Psychical Research Concerning Survival* (Sidgwick & Jackson, 1961), p. 230.

[3] Dr Martin Israel in *Life, Death and Psychical Research*, edited by J. D. Pearce-Higgins and G. S. Whitby (Rider, 1973), p. 262.

[4] Oscar Cullman, *Immortality of the Soul or Resurrection of the Dead?* (Epworth Press, 1958), pp. 10–11.

[5] F. W. Faber (1814–63). The quotation is verse 7 of his hymn 'My God, how wonderful thou art' (*Hymns Ancient and Modern Revised*, No. 169).

[6] See, for examples, E. J. Cotton, *They Need No Candle* (Churches' Fellowship for Psychical and Spiritual Studies, n.d. (1972)), Chapter 15, and J. A. Pike, as quoted on p. 54 above.

[7] *Hamlet*, I. v. 11–13.

[8] Albert Midlane, 1859; verse 3 of *Hymns Ancient and Modern Revised*, No. 452.

[9] J. A. T. Robinson, *Honest to God* (SCM Press, 1963), p. 13.

[10] H. H. Price, 'Survival and the Idea of "Another World" ', *Proceedings* of the SPR 50(1953), pp. 1–25, and reprinted in *Brain and Mind* (ed. J. R. Smythies; Routledge & Kegan Paul, 1965). A condensed version of this paper appeared in *Tomorrow* for Autumn 1956 (Parapsychology Foundation, Inc., NY) and was reprinted in *Does Man Survive Death?* (ed. Eileen J. Garrett; Helix Press NY and Holborn Publishing Co., London, 1958), pp. 37–44 and in *Man's Concern with Death* by Arnold Toynbee *et al.* (Hodder & Stoughton, 1968), pp. 251–6. The quotation above comes from pp. 11 ff. of the original paper and does not appear in the abbreviated version. The paper is discussed by H. D. Lewis in *The Self and Immortality* (Macmillan, 1973), esp. pp. 142–56. But Professor Lewis is wrong in saying that Price's paper was a *Presidential* Address to the SPR. Price was not the SPR's president that year. His paper was part of the Society's seventieth birthday celebrations, in 1952.

CHAPTER 9

[1] *Evil and the God of Love* (Macmillan, 1966; Collins Fontana, 1968), p. 112.

[2] Hick, *op. cit.*, pp. 112–13.

[3] M. F. Wiles, *The Remaking of Christian Doctrine* (SCM Press, 1974), p. 137.

[4] H. H. Price, *art. cit.*, (*supra*, p. 87). The extracts here printed occur on pp. 21–4.

[5] Neither condition, as critics of Price point out, is necessary; indeed, the almost complete subjectivity of the next world as here described is impossible to maintain if that world is peopled by other beings than one's self with whom one may have contact (H. D. Lewis, *The Self and*

Immortality (Macmillan, 1973), pp. 154 ff.). Professor Terence Penelhum has criticised Price's next world as 'solipsistic' (*Survival and Disembodied Existence* (Routledge & Kegan Paul, 1970), p. 51). The criticisms are not so damning if we hold that this description of the next world is a 'model' of a next world of interacting bodies, which Price develops in another part of his paper (see below, Chapter 11).

[6] H. D. Lewis (*op. cit.*, (n. 5 *supra*)), pp. 91–3 holds that this is not a fatal objection. There are many things which happened to us of which we retain no conscious memory.

[7] For examples, see Ian Stevenson, 'Twenty Cases Suggestive of Reincarnation', *Proceedings* of the American SPR, vol. 26(1966) and the review by John Beloff in *Journal* of the SPR vol. 44(1967), pp. 88–94; or C. T. K. Chari, 'Paramnesia and Reincarnation', *Proceedings* of the SPR vol. 53(1962), pp. 264–86.

[8] C. T. K. Chari, *art. cit.*n.7 *supra*. See also *H. D. Lewis (op. cit.* n.5 *supra*), pp. 98–103 for a battery of arguments against taking cases suggestive of reincarnation at their face value.

[9] As Anita Gregory has remarked, if out-of-the-body experiences 'are correlated with a substantial attenuation of bodily functioning, this would lend empirical support to the survival hypothesis' (*Journal* of the SPR, vol. 47(December 1974), p. 512, reviewing a paper by William Roll, 'A New Look at the Survival Problem', in *New Directions in Parapsychology*, ed. John Beloff, Elek Science, London, 1974).

[10] William Barrett, *Death-Bed Visions* (Methuen, 1926), p. 19 f; quoted from *Proceedings* of the SPR, 5(1888), p. 459.

[11] There is a useful collection of examples in Robert Crookall, *The Supreme Adventure* (James Clarke, 1961), pp. 10–49. See also C. E. J. Fryer, *A Hand in Dialogue* (Churches' Fellowship for Psychical and Spiritual Studies, 1975).

[12] Robert Crookall, *op. cit.*, pp. 42–7.

[13] *Ibid.*, pp. 38–41.

[14] As Matthew does in 8.12; 13.42,50; 22.13; 24.51 and 25.30. Luke uses the phrase only once (13.28) and the other evangelists not at all.

[15] 2 Thess. 1.9 (AV). The Greek is *olethros*, translated as 'ruin' in the *NEB* and 'destruction' in AV, RV and RSV.

[16] Translated by Edward Caswall from the seventeenth-century Latin. *Hymns Ancient and Modern Revised*, No. 106, verse 1.

CHAPTER 10

[1] *Funeral Hymns* (1759); *Hymns Ancient and Modern Revised*, No. 272, verse 2.

[2] Both these texts are here quoted in *AV*. The force of the Greek *koimaomai* is not brought out in the *NEB* translation.—see chapter 2, n.2.

[3] See, on this subject, I. T. Ramsey, 'Talking about God: Models, Ancient and Modern', in *Myth and Symbol* (SPCK Theological Collections, 7(1966), pp. 76–97).

[4] If we *must* find two words, I. T. Ramsey (following A. E. Hallett) suggests they might be 'eternal' and 'sempiternal', the latter meaning 'lasting for ever, being there always at every moment in time'. See his lecture 'The Concept of the Eternal', in *The Christian Hope* (SPCK Theological Collections, 13(1970), pp. 35–48.)

[5] *c.* 360 BC; section 37D.

[6] Rom. 6.22, referring to the *motif* of life through baptism introduced at 6.3.

[7] Read the whole of the sixth chapter of John, but note especially verse 54—'Whoever eats my flesh and drinks my blood possesses eternal life.'

[8] F. J. Taylor in *A Theological Word Book of the Bible* (ed. Alan Richardson; SCM Press, 1950), p. 128.

[9] *Confessions*, book 11, chapters 11, 13; translated by R. S. Pine-Coffin, in the Penguin Classics edition (1961), pp. 261, 263. Augustine wrote this about AD 398.

[10] *Timaeus* (*c.* 360 BC), section 37D–E. Translated by John Warrington in Dent's Everyman's Library edition (1965), pp. 30–1.

[11] G. D. Yarnold, *The Moving Image* (Allen & Unwin, 1966), p. 16. The whole of this book—though it makes stiff reading—is rewarding. Its analysis of time and eternity is most penetrating and draws together the concepts of science and theology in a suggestive and illuminating way.

[12] M. F. Wiles, *The Remaking of Christian Doctrine* (SCM Press, 1974), pp. 134 ff.

CHAPTER 11

[1] *c.* AD 200 in *De Resurrectione Carnis*, c. 35.

[2] See the form of the Creed printed in the Baptism service in the 1662 *Book of Common Prayer*. On the whole subject, see J. T. Darragh, *The Resurrection of the Flesh* (SPCK, 1921).

[3] *Faith*, stanza 11; from *The Temple*.

[4] Paul here was sharing the early Christian hope of an immediate end of the world, before the death of his own generation. Since his time we have had to learn to be more patient.

[5] See J. G. Davies, 'Factors Leading to the Emergence of Belief in the Resurrection of the Flesh', *Journal of Theological Studies* (n.s.) 23(1972), pp. 448–55; and Michael C. Perry, *The Easter Enigma* (Faber, 1959), pp. 103–19.

[6] Ignatius to the Smyrneans 3.1; to the Trallians, 9.2 (*c.* AD 107).

[7] G. W. H. Lampe and D. M. MacKinnon, *The Resurrection* (Mowbray, 1966), pp. 54, 58 f.

[8] Gerald O'Collins, *The Easter Jesus* (Darton, Longman & Todd, 1973), p. 96.

[9] J. G. Davies, *art. cit.*, p. 455.

[10] 1 Cor. 15.53; 2 Cor. 5.4. See C. F. D. Moule, 'St Paul and Dualism: the Pauline Conception of Resurrection', *New Testament Studies*, 12(1966), pp. 106–23.

[11] Quoted in *An Introduction to Western Philosophy* by Antony Flew (Thames & Hudson, 1971). See *Journal of Theological Studies* (n.s.), 23(1972), p. 558.

[12] J. A. T. Robinson, *The Body* (SCM Press, 1952), p. 28.

[13] See H. D. Lewis, *The Self and Immortality* (Macmillan, 1973), pp. 163–77 for an attempt to imagine such a state. In fact, he allows for communication between disembodied spirits; but only in a very attenuated form. M. F. Wiles (*The Remaking of Christian Doctrines*, SCM Press, 1974, p.140) points out that 'God is bodiless and inconceivable; but this is not (in Christian eyes at least) ground for denying his existence or regretting its form'. We ought not therefore to base arguments for the resurrection of the body on the inconceivability of a bodiless immortality.

[14] For some (perhaps over-fanciful) interpretations of mediumistic evidence on the characteristics of various kinds of 'body', see Robert Crookall, in *Life, Death and Psychical Research* (edited by J. D. Pearce-Higgins and G. S. Whitby; Rider, 1973), pp. 84 ff.

[15] Professor M. F. Wiles (*op. cit.*, p. 143) points out that we do not need to be able to *envisage* what is meant by 'body' after death in order to have a meaningful belief in life after death. No, admittedly. But it helps.

[16] Professor Price's speculations seem to describe a body which is more subjective than objective, and which belongs more to the person who perceives it than to the person who is being perceived. True; but it suggests one way of imagining how the body and the flesh can be thought of separately, and is confessedly only analogy. In a later form of his paper (ed. Garrett; see ch.8, n.10) he calls a body such as he here describes a 'dream body or image body' and then suggests that entities in the next world may be in an intermediate position between ordinary dream-images and ordinary material objects.

[17] As also do the speculations of Professor Price; see above, pp. 93ff.

[18] *Hamlet*, III. i. 65–8.

CHAPTER 12

[1] That is the attitude of Moses in Exod. 32.32. There is a converse attitude, given expression by Colin Morris on p. 21 of *Epistles to the Apostle* (Hodder & Stoughton, 1974): 'My mother-in-law lives with us, and frankly, makes my life a living hell. Jesus himself said that there are many mansions in heaven. Can I be assured that she will have separate accommodation, preferably in an entirely different wing?'

[2] F. H. Cleobury to M. C. Perry, 30 April 1969. Quoted with permission.

[3] J. A. T. Robinson, *In the End, God* . . . (James Clarke, 1950), pp. 89, 97.

[4] Homily 19; quoted on p. 70 of *Prayer and the Departed* (a Report of the Archbishops' Commission on Christian Doctrine), SPCK, 1971.

[5] See the résumé of arguments against the practice given as paragraph 10 of the report *Prayer and the Departed*, by the Archbishop's Commission on Christian Doctrine (SPCK, 1971), pp. 22–4.

[6] *Prayer and the Departed*, para. 9, pp. 19–20.

[7] *Ibid.*, pp. 20–1.

[8] J. V. Taylor (Bishop of Winchester, formerly General Secretary of the Church Missionary Society), *The Primal Vision* (SCM Press, 1963). See also A. C. Krass, *Go and Make Disciples* (SPCK, 1974), pp. 134–7.

[9] J. Paterson Smyth, *The Gospel of the Hereafter* (Hodder & Stoughton, 1910), p. 150.

[10] H. A. Williams, *Jesus and the Resurrection* (Longmans, 1951), p. 91 n.

[11] 'The Weight of Glory', *Theology*, November 1941, and repeated in several collections of Lewis's short pieces.

Index of Biblical References

Index of Names

General Index